ANGELIC TAILS

JOAN WESTER ANDERSON

ANGELIC
TAILS

TRUE STORIES OF
HEAVENLY CANINE COMPANIONS

LOYOLAPRESS.
A JESUIT MINISTRY
Chicago

LOYOLAPRESS.
A JESUIT MINISTRY

3441 N. Ashland Avenue
Chicago, Illinois 60657
(800) 621-1008
www.loyolapress.com

Cover image © Jimmy Bloomfield/Alamy

Library of Congress Cataloging-in-Publication Data
Anderson, Joan Wester.
  Angelic tails : true stories of heavenly canine companions / Joan Wester Anderson.
     p. cm.
  Includes bibliographical references.
  ISBN-13: 978-0-8294-3543-6
  ISBN-10: 0-8294-3543-3
1. Dogs--Religious aspects--Christianity--Anecdotes. I. Title.
  BT746.A535 2011
  231.7--dc22

                                                         2010048635

Printed in the United States of America
10 11 12 13 14 15 16 Versa 10 9 8 7 6 5 4 3 2 1

To Joseph Durepos,
Editor, agent, wise teacher, enthusiastic friend,
devoted dog lover.
You always have the best ideas!

CONTENTS

CONTENTS

INTRODUCTION

I

n 1991, after having been primarily a freelance magazine writer since my children were small, I decided to switch directions and write a book about angels. This topic was uncharted territory in those days; angels had been overlooked by the general population since the 1940s or thereabouts, and when noticed, they were usually presented in ethereal, theological terms. By contrast, my first angel book, *Where Angels Walk*, was a collection of down-to-earth true stories from ordinary people who believed they had been graced by a celestial being. In any given case, there was no way to *prove* that an angel had been involved, but the experiences themselves propelled the book to bestseller status, and I was flooded with new stories and requests for more books.

More angel books? What a joyful assignment! I didn't even have to decide on approaches or themes, for the fans themselves suggested a sequel titled *Where Miracles Happen*, outlining additional ways God communicated with people. Then along came a reader-requested volume for and about children and their unique relationships with guardian angels.

As I researched, asked questions, and wrote, my major challenge was making sure that everything presented was in line with biblical teaching. This was a sacred subject and must be conveyed in the most accurate terms possible. I asked the Holy Spirit for the gift of discernment, for help in selecting the appropriate material, and that there be no embellishment or "weirdness," just gentle guidance from heaven.

No shooting stars appeared. (They rarely do!) Instead, I came across a tender account of a woman who walked unknowingly through a dangerous area, but she felt her guardian angel's protection and arrived safely. Her "angel," it turned out, was a *dog*.

A dog! The story was terrific, but all wrong, I thought. Angels were heavenly beings, at the top of the spiritual heap. Dogs were . . . well, dogs. To merge the two might be offensive to some readers, even slightly heretical.

Yet, hadn't I asked the Holy Spirit for discernment? And hadn't it been established in earlier books that when angels appear to mortals, only occasionally do they wear the accustomed wings and haloes? I was discovering that more frequently they are disguised as ordinary people moving helpfully through a difficult situation, then disappearing before anyone realizes their true nature. If God would use anonymous spirits in human form to work his will, why not in dog form?

I learned that this had actually happened to St. John Bosco. As a minister to homeless boys, John was frequently mugged by the very kids he sought to help. At one point a large gray dog appeared at John's side, chasing away the gangs and keeping him safe. For years afterward, the dog would materialize when John was vulnerable, and it never showed signs of aging (talk about a miracle!).

Dogs certainly have played an important role in the protection and rescue of humans. In the Old Testament book of Tobit, a dog faithfully escorts Tobit's son Tobias and the archangel Raphael on their journeys. A thirteenth-century canine in France was venerated for years after miracles apparently took place at his shrine. A black-and-white dog (said by some to be a Dalmatian) is the symbol of the Dominican order of friars and nuns, who wear white habits with black capes. And who could overlook the loyal Saint Bernard, discovered by Swiss monks, whose loyalty and sense of smell helped to rescue lost travelers? *"For mine are all the animals of the forest, beasts by the thousands on my mountain,"* Psalms 50:10–11 reinforces this point of view. *"I know all the birds of the air, and whatever stirs in the plains belongs to me."* God told Noah that a rainbow was to be a reminder of the covenant between God and "every living creature on earth." St. Francis referred to animals as his "brothers and sisters."

I decided to use a couple of the dog stories I had collected in the next few books, perhaps to test the waters. Readers were delighted; not only did they support the appropriateness of a spiritual connection between humans and canines, but they also sent me more accounts of their own experiences. Why did they value their dogs so highly?

I was told that dogs sense and respond to a person's feelings and rarely complain. They live completely in the moment, unconcerned about what is to come. They wouldn't dream of judging us—they carry no hidden agenda, no fault-finding or vengefulness, and their devotion is fierce. If dogs were like people they would give up on us eventually, but they never do. If we could ask them why they love us so much, they would probably reply, "Just *because* . . ."

A dog will greet a stranger as if she is a best friend, spend all day listening, and never interrupt. If you are grieving, he will move into the pain, standing with you in your sorrow, and comforting you simply by his presence. (Author Matthew Fox considers his dog "my spiritual advisor.") A dog forces us to take a break, to slow down and enjoy our surroundings, and in doing so, we often connect with the mystical world beyond our own.

Interestingly, these descriptions reminded me of another category of creation: angels.

By now, my volumes had become a series, each containing at least one dog story, and more were waiting in the (you'll excuse the expression) wings. Perhaps the logical next step was to compile an entire book on the topic of dogs and how God uses them. As before, there would be stories from many points of view—a puppy who taught a child about faith, a ragtag mutt someone rescued just in time—the situations would be as varied as the canines themselves, but all would contain that sense of wonder, that heavenly connection: Look what God uses to make himself known to his children!

I began again to research and write, and here is the result. If an angel lover has the same impression I originally did, that a dog is simply a *dog*, I hope she reserves judgment. As she reads, she may come to see that the journey on earth is difficult at times, so our loving Father has provided many helpers for us. Friends, special teachers, gentle companions, and more.

Some may not fit the traditional mold. But a furry embrace and a cold nose work just as well.

Baby's Best Friend

You can't buy loyalty, they say,
I bought it, though, the other day.
You can't buy friendship tried and true
Well just the same, I bought that too.
I made my bid and on the spot
Bought love and faith and a whole job lot
Of happiness, so all in all
The purchase price was pretty small.
I bought a single trusting heart,
That gave devotion from the start.

If you think these things are not for sale,
Buy a brown-eyed puppy with a wagging tail.

—Unknown

Although Pam Sica and her husband, Troy, of Bellport, New York, had tried for ten years to have a baby, their efforts had failed. Pam was past forty now, and the doctors believed that her chance of becoming pregnant and delivering a healthy child was almost impossible. "Bullet, it looks like we're not going to have a baby after all." Pam held her golden retriever, Bullet, one afternoon as the tears came. She had gotten the dog when he was a tiny puppy and brought him into her marriage, and both she and Troy loved him dearly. In fact, at one point, they had almost lost him, too.

"When Bullet was twelve years old, we took him for his regular checkup, and his vet diagnosed both a heart condition and a tumor on his liver," Pam says. "The vet was afraid to operate just then because he wasn't sure Bullet's heart could take the anesthesia. So we waited until September, but by then the tumor had grown to the size of a baseball." Pam and Troy were told that it was time to let Bullet go. But Pam couldn't bring herself to do it. The dog had been a huge part of her life, and she was willing to fight for him.

The Sicas took out a $5000 loan to cover Bullet's operation and his other medical expenses. Friends and family thought they were insane. Weren't they already in financial difficulties due to their attempts to become parents? And now this expensive surgery on an elderly dog who probably wouldn't make it anyway. Pam knew what people thought. In fact, they were probably right. But love isn't always logical, and she would see Bullet through, whatever happened.

To everyone's surprise, Bullet survived the surgery and mended well. And in another year, there was a second shock. Pam and Troy had indeed beaten the odds. They were going to have a baby!

Pam had a difficult pregnancy, but on April 10, 2002, she delivered a healthy little boy, whom they named Troy Joseph. A day or two after the delivery, "I brought home a blanket from the baby's hospital bassinet and gave it to Bullet," Troy Senior recalls. "Despite his advancing age, he seemed delighted and scampered around like a pup, dragging the blanket beside him and sleeping with it at night." A few days later, when Pam and the baby came home, Bullet was ecstatic. He ran right to the baby, seeming to understand that little Troy was the newest member of his family. As the first few days passed, Pam realized that Bullet had appointed himself the baby's guardian and would come to alert her whenever Troy cried, even during the night.

Although motherhood took some getting used to, Pam's confidence grew. Bullet was like another adult, ready to caution or inform her about what the baby needed. How wonderful that he was able to share this time with her! Pam was even happier that she had listened to her own instincts instead of being persuaded to euthanize Bullet.

By the time three weeks had passed, life was settling into a comfortable routine. The baby usually had a bottle about 4:30 in the morning, and on the morning of May 1, Pam got up to prepare it, laying the baby on his back on their large bed, with pillows all around him and a single nightlight on. Troy went into the shower to get ready for work, and Bullet—Pam thought—was still drowsing near the crib. Lately he seemed to need more sleep.

But Bullet wasn't sleeping. Suddenly Pam heard him bark, and a few seconds later he came skidding down the hallway to the kitchen, ears flapping, whining urgently and insistently. "Bullet, stop!" Pam told him. "Do you want to go out?"

It was rare for Bullet to bark, even odder if he wanted to go out this early. But no. Bullet ran back down the hallway to the bedroom, then turned toward Pam. He looked up at her, and barked again, jumping off the floor, as if to say "C'mon!" Bullet was too old to be jumping. What was going on?

The baby! Suddenly Pam realized that Bullet was trying to alert her. She hurried after the dog, following him into the darkened bedroom. What she saw stunned her. Baby Troy's head was thrown back, and a raspy sound was coming from his throat. "Troy!" she screamed, tearing the drapes aside to let in some light. His face! As she watched, the baby's face changed from red to purple to blue—and then his tiny body went completely limp. SIDS? Sleep apnea? Was he choking? "Troy!" she screamed again, reaching for the phone.

Troy raced out of the shower, took in the frightening scene, and immediately began performing CPR on the baby. Pam called 911 but she was barely coherent. *God, God,* she kept thinking, *why would you give me a baby, and then take him back?*

Bullet was extremely upset. When the police and the paramedics came running up the stairs, Troy surrendered the baby to them, and the dog went berserk. This was *his* baby, he tried to tell these strangers, and no one else was supposed to get close! Bullet barked and whined the entire time the paramedics worked on baby Troy, but Pam was still close enough to hear one say quietly to the other, "We're losing him." It was like a nightmare that wouldn't end. *God, God,* she kept repeating.

The baby was rushed to Brookhaven Memorial Hospital in New York, where he was stabilized, and then he was sent on to Stonybrook, which had better facilities for treating sick infants. Thus, Pam was stunned when the baby relapsed twice, and a hospital official asked if she would be willing to donate his organs if he didn't survive. "I got hysterical again," Pam says. "I thought he was coming here to recover, not to die. It was too much trauma in such a short time."

They had not yet discovered why the baby was so sick. But at the end of that horrific day, the doctor who treated Troy had something important to tell them. "You were lucky to find him when you did. It takes only a few minutes for brain damage to set in with a very young infant." Pam and Troy looked at each other, stunned. They were just beginning to realize that Bullet's alert had saved their baby's life. Several years later, the couple happened to meet the paramedic who had answered the call that day, and he too remembered what a close call it had been. "What made you go to the baby's room?" he asked Pam. "In another few seconds, I think you would have lost him."

Baby Troy rallied and came home two weeks later, but he continued to have some mysterious symptoms until he was about eighteen months old. Then he was diagnosed with baby GERD, a gastrointestinal condition that is controlled with medication. The baby had also been born with a hole in his heart, but as he grew, the hole closed up by itself.

What can explain Bullet's awareness that the baby was in trouble that day? Experts say that dogs are often able to detect changes in atmosphere that humans miss. Or perhaps Bullet was used to Troy's normal breathing sound, and when it stopped, he sensed a problem. Pam agrees, but feels the explanation is obvious: "If we hadn't opted to save Bullet's life earlier, he wouldn't have been here to save Troy. That has to be more than just coincidence."

Little Troy's faithful companion, Bullet, had only one more year to share with him, and then the dog died peacefully one morning in Pam's arms. It was the way she had wanted it, but later she had some doubts. "I'm wondering if I made the right decision for Bullet," she confided to Troy Senior one hot August day on the patio. "What if he was suffering and I prolonged it?"

Troy looked around the yard, where Bullet had enjoyed so many pleasant years. If only dogs could talk! Then, suddenly, it started raining. "It poured for about a minute and stopped," Troy says. "Then the steam came up off the hot patio floor and formed a circle."

"Look!" Pam pointed. A huge yellow butterfly hovered in front of them, then flew right through the steam circle and over to the neighbor's tree.

The two looked at each other. The butterfly—a sign of new life. Was this an answer from Bullet?

Today Troy Sica is a healthy child and enjoys a happy life with his parents. He has learned to accept the many sightings of large yellow butterflies that seem to follow his family wherever they go. "Look, Mom!" he often says. "There's Bullet!"

Canine Sentries

We must remember that we have a Guardian Angel and turn to him in our thoughts and heart. This is good during peaceful times and especially so during turmoil.

—Bishop Theophan the Recluse

Nora doesn't want her real name used, "because I am still embarrassed at how naive I was." At that time, as a shy eighteen-year-old, she was caught up in romantic dreams. "More than anything, I wanted a man in my life," she says. "My best friend had just met someone special, and I longed for the same thing to happen to me."

Nora lived with her older brother Mark,* his wife, and their baby just outside a small Arkansas town, because it was

---

*not his real name

close to her job at a shoe factory. Sharing the house were three hounds, white with large black spots, which Mark used when he hunted quail and raccoons. The dogs were affectionate and rowdy, always jumping up on Nora, and she enjoyed playing with them. She babysat for her young nephew occasionally and attended church every Sunday. "I believed in God and the Bible," she says. "My mother always told me that if I ever got in trouble, I should ask God for help." Nora didn't anticipate trouble of any kind—in fact, *that* was the trouble! Although her life was pleasant, it seemed to be on hold.

One day a friend introduced Nora to a handsome young man. Nora liked Peter* right away, and when he invited her out for a casual dinner, she gladly accepted. But during dinner, Peter made several suggestive comments, and Nora became apprehensive. She was relieved when he drove her back to her brother's house. By then, it was dark.

"There was a little lane leading past the house, and Peter suggested we take a stroll before he left," Nora says. "I was hesitant since I knew my sister-in-law and the baby had gone to her

---

*not his real name

parents' for the weekend, and my brother was out hunting. But it was a beautiful, starry night." Peter held her hand, and despite her misgivings, Nora allowed romantic dreams to take over.

Before they had traveled more than a few yards down the quiet path, Peter suddenly attacked Nora, pushing her to the ground. He was tremendously strong and, horrified, Nora realized that she would be no match for him. Panic almost overwhelmed her, but then a thought flashed through her mind. God was watching her! He knew what was going on, he loved her, and he wouldn't desert her—her mother had said so.

"God, help me! Send help!" Nora cried out as she struggled. "God, please . . ." It seemed hopeless; Peter was overpowering her. But Nora continued to pray aloud. Words that she wasn't even thinking about poured out: *"God, help, help . . ."*

Suddenly Nora felt a presence. Looking up, she gasped. Mark's three black-and-white hunting dogs, outlined in moonlight, stood over them.

"Mark!" Was her brother nearby? Had he heard her scream? But there wasn't a sound. Nora knew that Mark's dogs would never leave his side. And these were definitely his dogs—she recognized their distinctive markings. But why had she not heard them approach? And why had they not barked and jumped upon her, as they always did?

Startled, Peter let go of her. He stared at the dogs, and the dogs stared back. One barked, once or twice, then quieted. The others stood mute, neither attacking nor retreating; they just stood there, like sentries. It was almost as if they understood what was going on and were looking on in eerie disapproval.

Peter got up and moved away, walking faster and faster as he headed back to his car. The dogs watched but stayed with Nora, encircling her. "You'll be all right now," they seemed to say. Shakily she rose to her feet. She *was* all right, except for her disillusionment. If it hadn't been for the dogs. . . . Slowly she started up the lane toward the house, looking back to see if they were following her. But the lane was empty. They must have returned to Mark. But where *was* Mark?

Several hours later, Mark finally pulled his truck into the driveway. Now the dogs were barking noisily, and when they

saw Nora they jumped out of the truck and leaped affection-
ately upon her, just as they always did, licking her face as if
she'd been gone for years. "Where have you been?" Nora asked
Mark as she warmed up some food for him.

"The dogs and I were coon hunting over in Finch tonight."

Finch was at least fifteen miles away. "*All* night?" Nora asked.

"We left about the same time you did," Mark explained.
"We've been up in the hills ever since."

The dogs couldn't have covered a fifteen-mile stretch to be
at her side. "Were the dogs with you the whole time?"

"The whole time, just like always."

Perhaps the animals she'd seen belonged to someone else.
No, Nora knew every hound in the area, and none looked
quite like Mark's. And what kind of dogs would be so silent,
so protective?

Mark was looking at her curiously. But she would need
some time to think before she could tell her brother—or anyone—about what she was beginning to believe. For if the dogs
that had rescued her were not Mark's or anyone else's, then
where had they come from? And who had sent them?

Today Nora is married and the mother of two. But she will never forget that night. "I think it was divine intervention," she says. "Angels do come in many forms." [1]

Maya the Magnificent

Dogs have given us their absolute all. We are the center of their universe. We are the focus of their love and faith and trust. They serve us in return for scraps. It is without a doubt the best deal man has ever made.

—Roger Caras, former president of SPCA

∾⧜∾

An estimated 25 percent of adult Americans suffer from a mental or emotional disorder in any given year, and depression is one of the most debilitating. Even children can be affected. Yet why would someone so young be so sad?

Deby Duzan of Springfield, Missouri, asked herself that question every day. Her daughter Sarah had lost interest in everything—family, school, friends, even animals (and she *loved* animals)—during the summer she was ten years old. "I chalked it up to growing pains and perhaps a bit of boredom," Deby remembers. "But when Sarah's moods continued, we went to the doctor." Sarah was diagnosed with depression and put on an antidepressant. But the diagnosis didn't help. "Now we knew *what* it was, but we didn't know how to cure it." Deby and her husband were baffled.

"My Dad was always willing to talk," Sarah, a self-proclaimed "Daddy's girl" says now, "and though he had never dealt with depression before, he always seemed to know what to say." But despite her parents' concern, nothing seemed to relieve Sarah for long. And to make matters worse, she hated her medication. She didn't think it helped much, and one of the side effects was weight gain. When school started up again, the kids began to make fun of her, which added loneliness to her burden. Friendless and disinterested in practically everything, Sarah struggled through school that year and then spent her summer sleeping, probably to escape the pain.

A pattern developed during the next several years, and although Sarah had an occasional pleasant day, there were more dark ones. Nothing seemed to comfort her for long, not even the two cats and the Great Dane that Sarah's family had adopted because of her love for animals. The worst time was in the middle of Sarah's junior year in high school. "She was so despondent that on three separate occasions she checked into a behavioral health center," Deby remembers. Despite her constant prayers, Deby despaired of ever finding an answer for her daughter.

By the time summer vacation arrived, however, Sarah was feeling well enough to make some changes in her life. She had tried several medications and now seemed to have found a winning combination. Hesitantly she applied for a job at the local pet store. "It's always scary to start a new job," she says, "but at least I felt I had some expertise and could actually help people with their pet questions."

Within weeks Deby saw a hopeful change in her daughter. Sarah had always loved animals, especially dogs (the bigger, the better), and her new job provided many of them to hug. She seemed more relaxed and happy than she'd been in years. She had even discovered the Bel-Rea Institute of Animal Technology in Denver, where she could learn to become a veterinary technician. Was this just another "up" phase? Or was Sarah on the road to a better life?

One summer morning, Sarah called Deby from the pet store. Kathleen, a woman who rescued dogs, had dropped off a large English mastiff, found abandoned in a house that a family had just vacated. "She's beautiful, Mom. Can I adopt her?" Sarah asked. "The fee is only thirty dollars."

An English mastiff. Weren't they about the size of a Shetland pony? The family already had a Great Dane—what if the dogs fought with each other? (Deby envisioned furniture and lamps flying through the air.) Mastiffs drooled too. And Sarah's father, already hip-deep in animals, wouldn't be thrilled about another. But Deby had heard the lilt in her daughter's voice, and she would do anything to keep it there. "Well, if you want to go to the Institute next year, a dog that big would certainly protect you," she heard herself saying.

Sarah cheered. She paid the adoption fee and brought Maya to the family vet. The vet estimated that Maya was about ten months old. She was underweight but otherwise in good shape. Sarah enrolled Maya in an obedience class right away, and she realized that the dog was very intelligent. "She does almost everything she's supposed to do," Sarah told her mother. And one day, at the vet's for another checkup, gentle Maya allowed the children in the waiting room to pat her. The vet noticed, too. "Maya is good with people," he pointed out. "You might want to consider training her to work as a therapy dog."

"I hadn't thought about that, but it sounded like a great idea," Sarah says. She found a trainer and started the classes necessary for Maya to be certified. Maya had some fear issues that needed to be worked out before the dog would be ready to do pet therapy. In the meantime, Sarah's senior year of high school began, and *she* had some fear issues, too. Deby was initially apprehensive. Would Sarah slip back into her sleep habit when confronted with the pressure of studying, working, plus caring for Maya? But it didn't happen. Sarah's depression occasionally surfaced, but she seemed to be able to cope with it and juggle her responsibilities more easily than she ever had. Maya, now weighing one hundred seventy-five pounds, took more than the usual adjustments, but as Sarah had predicted, everyone, even Dad, had learned to love this enormous newcomer.

Maya worked hard, and by the time she was ready to take the certification exam, Sarah seemed like a new person. The world was opening up to her, and she was determined to be part of it. Maya attracted attention when out for her walks, so Sarah overcame her shyness and began to introduce her dog to anyone who seemed interested. She took Maya to visit a nearby school, and was delighted when several teachers asked her to come back. "My mom taught in a middle school in a nearby town, and I developed an animal safety course for the kids," Sarah says. "It was basically to teach them how to approach a dog properly, how to care for their pets. . . . I would sometimes read books to them out of the Mudge series. Mudge books are about an English mastiff, so it was neat for them to have a 'Mudge' in the classroom." Sarah and Maya went to nursing homes too, and Sarah made it a point to talk with the residents, even those suffering from depression. She knew how that felt.

Maya was well behaved and sweet natured to everyone she met. And perhaps the most important beneficiary was Sarah herself. Somehow this drooly dog had made it easier for Sarah to bridge the gap, and live a normal life again. Deby didn't even hesitate when, after high school graduation, Sarah asked if she could become a foster parent for other large dogs.

Kathleen, the lady who had originally rescued Maya, was a good source for dogs that, they hoped, would eventually be adoptable. Sarah fostered a Saint Bernard and several Great Danes, teaching them basic obedience and behavior. But one day she came home with a question.

"Mom, I just discovered that the average fee to adopt an abandoned mastiff is $350. And most of them have some health problems."

"Three hundred and fifty dollars?" Deby was stunned.

"Even stranger, a mastiff puppy in good shape could cost as much as fifteen hundred."

The two looked at each other. There was no way that they could have afforded these fees. There was a funny little feeling in Deby's stomach as she thought back to the circumstances surrounding Maya's adoption.

Their friend Kathleen said she had "found" Maya in an abandoned house. And yet why, Deby wondered for the first time, would anyone have left this dog behind? When rescued, she was gentle, intelligent, and in reasonably good health. Further, if mastiffs were so expensive to adopt, why had Sarah been charged only a thirty-dollar fee?

Was Kathleen an "earth angel," someone who saw a young girl in need and somehow found a special dog to enter her life?

Or was the entire situation a blessing that heaven had arranged for her?

Sarah eventually finished her course work at the Bel-Rea Institute and decided to continue her education. Today she is studying medical technology and is the mother of a young son. She also has a Great Dane service dog that helps her handle her occasional anxiety. Life, she says, is good.

The women never discovered just how Maya was able to come into their lives, and the secret died with her in 2003. "I know Maya was a dog," Deby says, "but I think she was also a kind of angel. She came as an answer to prayer, didn't she?"

Sarah agrees. "I am still thankful for her every day," she says. "Maya gave me my life back."

OLD DOG, NEW TRICK

*Deafness: This is a malady that affects dogs when their person
wants them in and they want to stay out. Symptoms include staring
blankly at the person, then running in the opposite direction,
or lying down.*

—ANONYMOUS

The little ball of dirty white fluff was apparently frolicking on the railroad tracks in Kerns, Utah, that night when Fred Krause's freight train approached. It's the situation engineers dread most, and Fred and his conductor both froze. The two engines were pulling ten cars on a local run, and there wasn't enough time to stop. "I saw the dog on the rails ahead," says Fred, "but it was too late to do anything about it." As he passed over the furry pup, he knew it would have had no defense against the huge mass of steel, and the result was inevitable. "There's nothing you can do," he says. "It breaks your heart." Would someone be looking for this cuddly little mutt? Would they ever discover what had happened? Best to just put it out of his mind.

Fred made his delivery at Kennecott Copper Mine, the only stop on this sixteen-mile route, and started his return trip. "Normally on a Sunday night we would have picked up cars from other trains, and then proceeded on to Provo. We almost never do a Kennecott flip (a run up to Kennecott and back) without a trip to Provo." Fred remembered where the accident had occurred. As he approached the spot, he slowed down. A mile, another mile, and then . . . Wait! Fred leaned forward. What was that, trotting toward him down the tracks?

Fred could hardly believe his eyes. By the flare of the engine light, he saw the white dog, alive and unscathed! He must have scooted between the rails, and the train had probably passed right over him without doing any harm. However, like a bad dream, it was all happening again! "Come on, buddy, get off the tracks!" Fred flashed the lights, blew the whistle, and tried to slow down, but the dog scampered *toward* the engine.

Right before it hit him, Fred got a clear look at the dog. "Oh, no!" he shouted. "It's a Shih Tzu!"

Fred and his wife have a Shih Tzu, seven-year-old Milo.

Everything was happening so fast, and then the train ran over the dog. Fred heard an unmistakable sound, the thud of something hitting the snow plow mounted on the front of the engine. If he hadn't been crushed, the stray would have been struck by the plow. Either way, it was definitely over.

The train sped on, but Fred couldn't stop thinking about the dog. It was 11 p.m. when his shift ended, and as he was pulling out of the parking lot, he made a decision. "I had convinced myself that no dog could survive an impact with the train, but this was going to be my only chance to know for sure. That's when I decided to go back." He drove his car to a site that he judged to be close to where the dog had been hit. Taking along his flashlight, he walked down the rails, calling and whistling in the darkness. He felt himself being prodded to go just a little farther, and then a little more. Then he saw a forlorn ball of matted fur lying between the tracks. Fred shone the light on the little pile. The pile quivered, got up on all fours, turned around, and looked at Fred as if to say, *What took you so long?*

Fred was stunned. "The last thing I expected was to find him alive," he says. But it was another chance, and Fred couldn't abandon him now, not after all that had happened. Instead, the two went to the vet emergency room.

The "little guy," as Fred had already named him, was about ten years old, and in a somewhat dazed condition. His encounter with the train's snowplow had left him with only a concussion, no broken bones or any other damage. However, he had probably been homeless for some time, since his fur was matted, and he had infections in his eyes and feet. (The eye problems may have accounted for him running toward the train instead of away from it.) But it seemed obvious that someone had loved him up until the recent past. He was also hungry, so after the amazed vet had released him, Fred brought him home for breakfast. His wife, Lori, was astonished at the story.

Later that day, the area experienced a major snowstorm, and Fred realized that if he hadn't rescued the dog when he did, given his injuries, the freezing weather, and the fox population, the little guy would not have lived much longer. "I have hit a few dogs in the past," Fred says, "but I've never gone back to check on any of them. It's too difficult. Why I did this time,

I just don't know." And was it mere coincidence that his run that night kept him in the vicinity of the little guy, rather than miles away in Provo? Once again, the timing had been perfect.

An owner never showed up, so Fred and Lori decided to adopt their invalid, after convincing Milo that it might be fun to have a pal. And Little Guy is delighted with his new digs.

"I must admit that I am not a spiritual person," says Fred, "but Lori and I both agree that there almost seems to have been some sort of 'divine intervention' in this particular situation, so many details that never or very seldom occur, that happened that day. It's enough to make someone like myself go, 'Hmmmm, I wonder . . .'"

CANINE CORPORAL

DOG, n. A subsidiary Deity designed to catch the overflow and surplus of the world's worship.

—AMBROSE BIERCE, *THE DEVIL'S DICTIONARY*

As the Vietnam war heated up, then-eighteen-year-old Pat "Pitbull" Dugan thought about enlisting. After all, he came from a long line of macho men in Del Rio, Texas. His grandfather and great-grandfather worked in law enforcement, and his father, Charles, had been a survival instructor in the U.S. Army Air Corps during World War II. Charles, in fact, had been shot down behind enemy lines in Italy but had escaped and heroically led his crew to safety. As Pat grew up, he hung on his father's words and lessons, even learning how to navigate without using a map. He imagined himself following in the family footsteps and, after a substandard semester at college, decided to go ahead. A good friend, Mykle Stahl, enlisted with him.

His father was furious when Pat announced his decision, but ironically, it had been Charles's own patriotism that had impressed his son so much and had given him the temperament he would need to survive.

In Vietnam, Pat was part of a hand-picked group whose specialty was intelligence. "A reconnaissance Marine goes out and gathers information to save lives," he says. "Where the enemy is, their troop strength, natural hazards—these are the things we needed to know." The information was collected on patrols, in jungles so overgrown that the men might not see the sun for days. Nor could they walk on trails because most were booby trapped. During hundreds of combat missions, Pat got to know the people in small villages. He talked with the children and brought American cigarettes. And it paid off. "Sometimes the women would warn me, with their facial expressions, 'no, don't go that way, go this way.' Of course one never knew who was a friend, and who was just appearing as one."

One day Pat came upon a small brown puppy being fattened up for a villager's meal. Since his family had always had dogs, Pat couldn't pass up this one. He rescued the pup and introduced it to his platoon. Brown Dog was later responsible for saving several Marines, when he went "on alert" in the bunker. (The enemy was involved in a sneak attack and none of the Americans would have heard anything in time.) During the battle, Brown Dog was hit by shrapnel, and Pat put him on a medivac helicopter. The pup needed more than one hundred stitches, but he was saved by Army veterinarians. He resumed his job, receiving a promotion to Corporal Brown Dog. Later he was passed to the Marines that followed. "I tried to bring Corporal Brown Dog home with me," Pat says, "but these were different times, and America didn't even bring all of our own scout/guard dogs home."

Life in Vietnam had been physically difficult and emotionally draining. Despite everything, Corporal Patrick Dugan returned home safely as a highly decorated combat veteran, finished college, got married, and became a teacher, later the principal of Del Rio High School. He also worked in law enforcement as a federal parole officer, doing narcotics interdiction along the Mexican border. But as Pat will tell you, "Once a Marine, always a Marine." So in addition to his other jobs, he stayed involved in the reserves as a survival instructor, as his father had done, and also rewrote a survival manual. At one point, Pat was given an award for his work, presented by his buddy Colonel Mykle Stahl, who had opted for a career in the military.

Given his strong patriotism and lifelong commitment to the Marines, Pat did not find it difficult to talk about his experiences, as so many vets did. The prevailing wisdom at the time said that it was best to put memories behind him and move on with his life. Yet, few civilians were aware of the traumas that many Vietnam vets were quietly handling, or not handling. Depression, bouts of mysterious illnesses, rising rates of family breakups—like a silent blight, these problems seeped into the population. The vets coming home were not treated as the heroes they were because the war was unpopular; activists insulted them and encouraged the public to turn away. Pat had always believed that the courage and bravery of everyone who has served in the military needs to be honored. But there were few expressions of thanks. It was in this atmosphere that he readjusted. He had discovered that if he had a dog nearby, he could better manage his own occasional stress. Keeping busy was another helpful tool, especially when Lucky came into his life.

Lucky was a pit bull, the runt of a litter who was being maltreated by drug dealers. Pat was attempting to bust a drug and robbery ring, and when he saw the dog, he rescued him. "I named him Lucky because he was indeed lucky that I came along." Although there were other dogs in his family, he and Lucky were inseparable as the years passed.

Pat did not go gently into retirement. He had been living at a hundred miles an hour, he says, and when it suddenly came to an end and leisure prevailed, he couldn't adjust. Then the unthinkable happened: Lucky died. Pat, already struggling to cope with emerging depression, felt it was the last straw. "I didn't want to love anymore," he admits. "The day I buried Lucky, I felt like jumping into the ground myself." He frequently sat by the grave, grieving deeply. Lucky had been one of a kind, and Pat was not going to risk being hurt again.

Pat continued his daily walks without a canine companion. In Del Rio, four cemeteries abut one another, like an oasis in the midst of the desertlike environment, offering an abundance of wildlife and greenery. Pat often trudged these quiet paths. One morning a fog was so dense that he could hardly see, and he detoured through a park instead. Up ahead he caught a glimpse of white. Pat squinted into the mist as he drew closer. Then he saw that it was a Jack Russell terrier. No collar, no identification tags, a little brown spot over one eye. Pat had no idea where it had come from.

But he did know that Jack Russells are intense, high energy dogs. Why was this one sitting calmly on the walking track, as if *waiting* for Pat? "I picked him up, and I felt a little spark," almost a sense of recognition. His no-dog policy had just been abandoned.

Pat took the dog to his vet, then temporarily to a friend's house. If he was going to keep this dog, he would need to introduce him gradually to the other pets at home. The whole scenario seemed odd; it was almost as if the dog had known Pat would be passing by. Yet if it hadn't been for the fog, rare in that area, he wouldn't have been walking on the track at all.

Although Pat circulated notices to radio stations, vet offices, and the dog pound, no one stepped forward to claim this handsome dog. The day that Pat introduced his new companion to the other household pets, expecting a possible free-for-all, the other dogs barely reacted. Again, it seemed almost eerie, as if the newcomer had always lived there. "He jumped upon my bed that first night, and has been there ever since," says Pat. Sensing that something a bit out of the ordinary was happening, Pat named the terrier Corporal J.R. Dugan, USMC 2164539. "I gave him the combination of the initials for his breed, Jack Russell (J.R.) with my U.S. Marine Corps rank and serial number," Pat says, "because I was already realizing he had the heart of a lion." The dog would be called Corporal J.R. Dugan or J.R, for short. If people wondered why, Pat would be glad to explain.

Time passed, and Pat fell more and more in love with J.R. The terrier was a perfect companion, glued to Pat's side, and very affectionate. He, too, enjoyed the daily walks through the cemeteries. Plant and bird life populated this oasis, and J.R. missed nothing. Instead of barking, however, he would alert Pat by making eye contact whenever he sensed a presence nearby, and Pat would then reach for his binoculars to enjoy the discovery. J.R. also had a signal when he wanted water and usually led Pat to a little bench where the pair would take a break. In fact, J.R. often seemed to know what Pat was thinking. In this peaceful atmosphere, Pat began to reflect, allowing memories to surface, taking time to face things he had previously avoided thinking about. Maybe there was something to this retirement after all. Slowly, with J.R. in mute encouragement, he began to heal.

On November 10, the official birthday of the U.S. Marine Corps, the weather was chilly and overcast as Pat gathered some American flags to put on his father's grave. He and J.R. walked in the cemetery for an hour afterward, until J.R. requested water. Pat headed for the nearest bench, but J.R. pulled against the leash. It was obvious that he wanted to go in another direction, which was unusual for him. Pat gave in and let J.R. lead. The dog pushed forward to a section they had never visited.

There was another bench up ahead, and when they reached it, Pat sat down to get some water out of his pack. J.R., however, still wanted to move on. He was insistent, almost like a dog with a mission. "I gave him a lot of leash, and he finally stopped at a grave several yards away, covered by years of dirt, leaves, and neglect." J.R. had never paid any attention to graves or headstones before. Now, however, he started to scratch at the pile of debris, scattering dirt everywhere. Was there something under the waste attracting his attention? Pat stood up and started to rein in the dog. It was then he realized that J.R. was digging at a military grave.

J.R. stopped and met Pat's eyes, almost as if he was pleading for help. Well, if it was that important. . . . "I got down on my knees and started to help J.R. scrape the dirt from the stone," Pat says. As the final layer gave way, J.R. stopped and assumed a rigid pose, staring at the marker, almost as if he were standing at attention. Puzzled, Pat read the tombstone's inscription:

> JACK A. RUSSELL
> TEXAS
> CPL SIGNAL CORPS
> JULY 21, 1928 – JULY 16, 1952

It seemed as if all time and motion had frozen. Except for the dog. Pat watched as Corporal J.R. deliberately laid his head on both paws and rested on the stone of another Corporal J.R., killed in the Korean War. Were these two linked? Had they met in another time or place?

Pat faced the questions he had never confronted: Was it likely that, in such a small town, no one had ever seen J.R. before Pat encountered him? Was it simply a coincidence that the perfect dog had come to him at the perfect time? Then he realized that, all his life, he had been rescuing people and animals, anything God sent him. Now God was letting him know—on a most significant day—that his labors, his pure heart, his sacrifices, and even his losses had been seen and appreciated. He was and always had been a hero in God's eyes.

Corporal J.R. was making eye contact with him now, and Pat understood the message: the two of them would clean and restore this precious gravesite, for every veteran deserves his place in the sun. And as they worked together, Pat would marvel at the meaning of it all. However it had happened, this little pup had taught him to love again.

DOGGONE DARLING

Dachshunds are ideal dogs for small children, as they are already stretched and pulled to such a length that the child cannot do much harm one way or the other.

—ROBERT BENCHLEY

⌖

When Colt Urquhart of Kennewick, Washington, set out with his friend Josh for a day of fishing, he had no inkling what he would catch. The men were up to their knees offshore on a lake when one of them spotted something small, brown, and wiggly struggling toward them underwater. It was a puppy! Quickly Colt scooped it up. It was a little dachshund, obviously running out of strength to keep paddling. If the men hadn't come along, it wouldn't have lived much longer.

The puppy was shivering, so Colt tucked him inside his shirt. "We've got to find his owner," he told Josh, who agreed. Someone among the hikers and picnickers must be awfully concerned right now. But oddly, as they walked from family to family holding up the dog, no one seemed to be missing one. An older couple admitted that they had shooed it away because it had gotten into their belongings, and they had seen the pup scamper into the water. With its stubby legs, the pup had run out of solid ground very quickly. Colt had to get it warm and fed. Both men lived in trailers, but Josh had more room, so he took the dachshund home.

As it happened, Josh couldn't keep the dog. His park owner had a rule against having any pets. "Ours didn't," Colt's wife, Diane, says, "and over the years we have taken in lost dogs and kept them until their owners came." But this dachshund was very small, and might not have anyone looking for him. Perhaps they would end up keeping him. "We had a family meeting, and the vote was yes," says Diane. Sure, they had heard all the jokes about "wiener dogs." But this one seemed especially sweet natured, and it loved to cuddle—just the kind of dog children need.

They named him JoJo, and he settled in without much trouble. The kids soon noticed that his ears usually expressed his feelings. "When happy, he does a perky droop, when hungry, his ears are gathered at the top of his head," says Diane. "When in trouble or embarrassed, they are out and fanned— we call them elephant ears." Jojo was simple to read, which made his care even easier. In fact, as the months went on, he developed a bit of an attitude, as if he were in charge of the family. He was fiercely protective of the children, and chose then-eight-year-old Kalen as his bunkmate. They soon slipped into a routine: JoJo would sleep with Kalen but would come out every hour or so to check on Colt and Diane as they watched television. "If we were up too late for his liking, he would wait patiently at our feet, until we went to bed," Diane says. If the couple stayed up later than JoJo thought acceptable, he would sigh dramatically and return to Kalen's room in defeat. In an hour or so, he would be back to prod Colt and Diane again.

But the pattern changed one evening in February of 2010. It was past midnight, the trailer was quiet, and Diane and Colt were watching the end of a movie. JoJo came out of Kalen's room, somewhat agitated. The adults were surprised. "Jojo had been fed and had already gone outside," Diane says. "It wasn't like him to be busy and up so late." Diane told him to go back to bed and, being the obliging pooch that he was, he obeyed.

But only for a few moments. Then he appeared again, almost pacing. "If a dog can look worried, he did," Diane says. Jojo went back and forth four times, each time returning to Kalen's room. It was then that Diane noticed his ears. They were straight down, which in some breeds denotes danger.

By now, the drowsy couple realized that something was wrong. JoJo had returned to Kalen's room, and when they entered, the dog was on her bed, shoving his nose against her and trying to wake her up. "We didn't see anything out of the ordinary," says Diane, "but then I smelled an odor of burning rubber." And when she touched the wall at the head of Kalen's bed, it felt hot. Colt yanked the alarm clock and lamp out of the wall, and a puff of smoke followed. "Get out!" he yelled. Quickly he awakened the children while Diana phoned 911. Grabbing their two cats and JoJo, the family fled.

Firefighters arrived quickly. Diane, the children, and the animals waited in their car while Colt took the firemen into the trailer to show them where the smell was coming from and where the electricity could be shut off. "When they came out, they told us that Kalen's outlet was minutes away from catching fire," Diane says. Holding their children and pets closely, the couple looked at each other. There had been no smoke or flames, no injuries or even deaths, because of JoJo. The bossy little dog with the short stubby legs had saved his entire family.

JoJo continues to be an absolute treat of a dog, says Diane. "I am forever grateful that he floated by my husband and Josh, so we could share his precious life."

TO SIR, WITH LOVE

Behold, I send my angel before you to guard you along the way and to bring you to the place I have prepared. Give him reverence and listen to him; and if you heed his voice, I will be an enemy to your enemy and a foe to your foes.

—Exodus 23:20–22

⟡

Bill and Marcia Holton and their three children lived on a wheat ranch in Oregon; Marcia's parents, Verne and Kay, lived next door. The two family homes were at the bottom of Juniper Canyon, with some of the wheat fields on top of the hill behind the houses. "Our neighbors out here are spread apart, and the nearest small town is Helix, ten miles from our ranch," Marcia explains. Sometimes it seemed as if they were the only people on earth. Occasionally Marcia got a little lonely, but she was a woman of faith who prayed regularly that God would watch over her family. So far God had not disappointed her.

It was a beautiful Sunday afternoon in early spring, and Marcia had flung open the kitchen door, put boots on the kids so they could run wherever they wanted, and gone outside with them. The sun and promise of warmth were all around them, and planting had begun. Marcia loved this time of year.

"Mommy, look!" Her six-year-old was pointing to the top of the hill behind the house.

Marcia gasped. There was an animal the size of a minivan up there, sitting calmly and looking down at them. It was huge, at least two hundred pounds. A bear? Marcia thought not—its fur was yellow and fluffy. A mountain lion? "Walk real slowly toward the house," she whispered to the children. "Wait there, and don't come back until I tell you."

Then Marcia took a careful step toward the animal. She knew she would have to investigate it before she'd feel safe letting the children play outside again.

As she got closer, Marcia could hardly believe her eyes. It was a dog! The biggest dog she had ever seen, probably part mastiff, part Saint Bernard. Where had he come from? She knew all the dogs in the Helix area, and no one owned one like this. Was he friendly? "Here, boy . . ." she put out a tentative hand.

As if he had been given permission, the dog got up and trotted down the hill, directly to Marcia, tail sweeping the driveway. He allowed himself to be petted, his ears to be scratched and—once she had called the children over to him— hugged and ridden on. "Isn't he nice?" Marcia said. "What shall we name him?"

"I think we should call him 'Sir'," one of the children suggested. "Because he deserves respect."

He did seem regal. Now all that was needed was Bill's permission to keep him. The family could hardly wait until he got home from plowing.

"Oh, come on—he won't eat much," Marcia teased that night. "Look at him—isn't he cute?"

"'Cute' isn't quite the word I'd use," Bill responded. Sir reminded him more of the lions he had seen in zoos.

"But he seems to know us, Daddy," the five-year-old pointed out. "As if he's always lived here." Everyone stared at

Sir, who seemed to be following the conversation, his massive head moving from one person to another.

"Well . . ." Bill was definitely weakening. Although his in-laws had two blue-heeler dogs to help with the cattle they raised, Bill's family didn't own one. Yet what better place for such a big dog than a ranch? "But we'll have to advertise in the 'Lost and Found' in case he belongs to anyone," Bill said. "And if we have to give him back, I don't want you all to be sad." Everyone cheered and agreed.

This cabbie probably didn't know it was his final Sunday on earth, Paul Smith* mused, as he lounged in the back seat, his pistol pointed at the hijacked driver's head. But he wasn't going to leave any witnesses to this last robbery. The clerk in the Walla Walla convenience store hadn't seen his face—he'd locked her in the storage closet before he emptied the cash register. But it wasn't much cash, and he was going to have to pull another job soon.

_____

*not his real name

Most important, however, was finding a spot where he could hide for a while. He was an escaped convict on the run, and out here in Oregon the little homesteads were so few and far between that he could easily dispose of the residents, then portray himself as a visiting relative or friend if any nosy neighbor happened by. Eventually he'd commandeer another car and driver, just like this one, and set out again, working his way east. The police would never find him if he stayed out of sight for a while.

The cab driver's hands were shaking. "I-I know you told me not to talk," he said, "but we've gone sixty miles and my gas gauge is on E. I was already low when you pulled the gun on me . . ."

Paul Smith looked out the window. They were passing a wheat field, which looked down into a canyon. At the bottom were two houses. He could see no other dwellings around for miles in any direction. Perfect. He could wait up here until dark. "Turn into this field," he told the driver, who obeyed just as the engine began to sputter. If anyone in those houses did hear the shot, Smith reflected, they would probably assume it was just a hunter bringing down a rabbit. He looked at the terrified cabbie and reached for his gun.

It was a perfect set-up; later, from his perch on top of the hill, he watched the families move about the two houses. At times, it looked as if the two women and the little kids were alone. He considered strategies. He could go down now, surprise and overpower the women and children, or he could wait until dark when the men would probably be back, break into one of the houses and take command of everyone at the same time. But he couldn't afford to make a mistake in judgment, because he had very few bullets left. Ultimately, he had to get far away from here, before the authorities in Washington figured out where he had gone.

It would have to be tonight, when they were asleep and unprepared.

Meanwhile, the Holtons were debating on whether Sir should sleep in the house or the barn. But the massive canine settled down easily on the porch across the back door threshold, as if he'd always done so. There was no point in trying to move him, and quiet eventually descended on the Holton household. Until a little after midnight. Then Sir started to bark. At first it was just a few short yaps, followed by growling, then howling.

"Sir, stop it!" Bill called through the open screened window.

Sir obeyed, but a few minutes later the whole process started again.

"What is the matter with that dog?" Bill asked irritably. He got up again and looked out the windows of the porch door. There was no sign of a wild animal. It wasn't that unusual for a coyote or badger to run through the yard and set off a brief chorus of barking from the dogs next door. But tonight their in-laws' dogs were absolutely quiet.

"Maybe he's homesick," Marcia suggested.

"Wouldn't he be whining?" Bill asked. "This sounds more like aggressiveness. Sir, be quiet!"

Again, Sir obeyed, but only for a moment. He refused to leave the back door, to go in search of what was bothering him. But he also barked and growled continuously, as if he were keeping something at bay. It was almost dawn before the adults in the two households all fell asleep. "None of us were very happy with Sir or me that morning," Marcia recalls. "But we all agreed to try him one more night."

That day Marcia and the children played with Sir continuously. Wherever they went on the ranch—into the barn, across the road—he accompanied them. "When we were in the house, Sir would lie in front of the door. Nothing could get him to move, until we came out of the house again."

That night, Sir barked only a few times. Marcia relaxed. He was settling into his new home, and she was delighted about it. She loved him and depended on him already in a way she had never thought she could.

A few days later, Marcia's dad, Verne, was on his way to town when he passed one of the wheat fields and saw something shining, looking like a car windshield. There shouldn't be any cars there. Verne drove closer until he spotted a taxi with Washington state license plates on it. Something was definitely wrong, but he wasn't about to investigate by himself. He turned around, drove home, and called the state police. "Get your family, your rifle, and lock yourselves in one of the houses. And don't open the door for anyone," he was told. The police were on their way.

Slowly, over the next several hours as the authorities investigated, Marcia, Bill, and their folks absorbed the shocking story. On Sunday an escaped convict who had just robbed a convenience store had forced a cab driver to take him just past Helix, to their own wheat farm, where he then murdered the cab driver.

The sheriff took Marcia and Bill up the hill, about 100 feet from their back porch, and pointed to footprints, several cigarette butts, and a discarded cigarette package. Marcia was shocked. The killer had obviously stood here in the dark, waiting for a chance to come down and . . . she didn't want to think about it.

But why hadn't he done so? "I think the only thing that saved all of you was that dog sticking to you like glue," said the sheriff. "If Smith was running low on bullets and had to get past Sir's attack before he could get to you . . ."

"He'd also lose the element of surprise," Bill commented. He had complained about Sir's noisiness. But what would have happened to all of them if Sir had not warned the criminal away? What would have happened if they had not adopted Sir?

No one knew where Paul Smith had gone. Later, it was discovered that he had flagged down another farmer, taken him hostage, and repeated the scenario across the country. He killed one more person before he was caught in Pittsburgh about a week after he had left the Holton farm. Immediately he was sent back to prison in Washington. Sir stayed with the Holtons for about a year before everyone sensed that it was time for him to move on. Ultimately, he went to live at the fire station in town.

Why was the Holton family spared, and not the unfortunate hostages? Another mystery, for we know that God loved them all. But "In the Bible, it tells us that if we pray, God provides angels for our protection," Marcia says. Perhaps Sir was not really an angel. But that he was sent from heaven, Marcia has no doubts.[2]

VIEWS FROM THE BRIDGE

You think dogs will not be in heaven? I tell you, they will be there long before any of us.

—ROBERT LOUIS STEVENSON

D o dogs go to heaven? There's an Internet legend among dog lovers about Rainbow Bridge, a mythical place between heaven and earth, where dogs wait for their masters to join them for all eternity. In more theological discussions, the point is frequently raised that dogs may indeed have souls, although lower in the ranking than humans'. Animals, as part of God's creation, were declared "good" (Genesis 1:25) and by their mere existence they bless God and give God glory. Author Ptolemy Tompkins, writing in *The Divine Life of Animals*, points out that "nothing of what we love down here on earth is ever truly lost. . . . Though this world is imperfect and fallen, there exists a place where the pain of that imperfection will be healed. Not just for humans, but for every creature, great and small."

What do we conclude? Perhaps we simply listen to the stories.

Dr. Candace Williamson Murdock of Rome, Georgia, had just had a miscarriage. The night after she returned from the hospital, she stayed awake, restless and upset. This baby had not been her first, but like all children, it was irreplaceable, and she grieved deeply at the loss. "Suddenly a scene appeared—as if it was on a movie screen—right in front of me," Candace recounts. She blinked, but the vision remained.

It was a sunny green meadow. In its midst were dogs playing and chasing each other, crossing her vision toward the right side. "The dogs seemed somehow familiar," she says. "I suddenly realized that they were our family pets, dogs from my childhood!" Watching intently, Candace saw her father running into the center of the scene, the dogs leaping joyfully about him. Her father had been killed in a plane crash seven years ago. He had raised and loved many dogs in his lifetime.

Then Candace realized that her father was not alone. He was gripping the hand of a small blond child. They were looking toward the right. Candace's father seemed to be pointing at something, as if he were explaining it—and both were smiling. Instantly Candace knew this child was the baby she'd just lost. Obviously her father was welcoming the child into heaven, and God had allowed her to witness it so she would be consoled.

"I cannot explain how much comfort this vision gave me," Candace says. "I had never experienced anything like it, nor would I have pictured heaven in this way, but I was *not* hallucinating. To know that my child, my father, and his beloved dogs were all together was the best answer to prayer that I could have asked for. God does care."[3]

⚬⚭⚬

Mary Ellen Hansburg, of Columbus, Ohio, was pleased and proud when her daughters, Eliza and Lilly, went off to different colleges, each wearing an unmistakable badge of confidence and anticipation. Wasn't this what she had hoped for? Yet Me (it's what everyone calls her) missed the girls terribly. She was sure that Waddles, the family dog, did too.

Waddles, a brown and white terrier-sheltie mix, was small in size, but he had a huge and loving heart. He had been the girls' joy and comfort since their childhood and was very sensitive to the moods and nuances of their lives. He seemed to know if anything was amiss, and he could raise a ruckus if he felt one of the girls was distressed or needed defending.

Me was a teacher, and the same autumn her daughters went to college, Me returned to the classroom. She was pleased that the fall quarter was unfolding with its pleasures and challenges. One early morning as Me drove to school, she cast a sideways glance out the passenger window. There was Waddles, running along the shoulder of the highway! "He was running hard and panting, so I slowed down and watched as he slowed down too." What was he doing out here on the road?

Finally able to pull over, Me looked to see where Waddles was. That dog was always full of surprises. But Waddles was gone—vanished. This left Me a bit apprehensive and edgy. She wondered about her daughters. Was Waddles bringing her a message? Was everything all right with them?

Arriving at school, she sent off a quick email to each of them, asking in a general way if all was okay. Later that day, each girl called her and left a message:

"Mom, good to hear from you. Keep me in your prayers— lots of challenges," relayed Eliza, a senior.

"Hey, thanks. I do want to talk and will call back today," said freshman Lilly.

Indeed, as Me later learned, each of the girls was facing demanding situations in their classes, and a reassuring conversation with Mom was just what they had needed. Relieved, Me was so glad she had contacted each one.

She reflected on all of this while pulling into the driveway at the end of the day. The vague fears she sometimes had about letting her daughters go had disappeared. Instead she felt confident and ready to get on with her life. Thank goodness for Waddles and the signal he sent. Me knew that their special little dog had not been on the highway today, because he had died almost a year ago. But he had sent her the message she needed most. "Waddles had always been the girls' playmate and protector. He still is, just this time from the other side of the Rainbow Bridge."[3]

ROCH

Prayer for Animals

Hear our humble prayer, O God, for our friends, the
*   animals,*
Especially for those who are suffering;
For any that are hunted or lost or deserted or frightened
*   or hungry.*

. . .

We entreat for them all thy mercy and pity,
And for those who deal with them.
We ask a heart of compassion, and gentle hands and
*   kindly words.*
Make us, ourselves, to be true friends to animals
And so to share the blessings of the merciful.

—ALBERT SCHWEITZER

Is there a patron saint of dogs and dog lovers? (Patron saints are advocates and defenders of certain nations, places, activities, occupations, or ages). According to most historians there is indeed: St. Roch (also known as Rock, Rocco, Rollox, Rouque and Rochus—you get the idea). Tradition says that Roch was born into a wealthy family in Montpellier, France, around 1295. His father was governor of the city. At birth, people noticed Roch was marked on his chest with a red cross. (In later years, it would be considered a sign of his holiness.) He was given every material advantage and it was expected he would step into his father's position at the proper time.

However, Roch was developing a heart for the poor, and he was concerned about the homeless and the sick. When he was twenty, his parents died, and, instead of becoming governor, he distributed his fortune to the needy and left for Rome. On the way, he passed many towns where the plague had taken hold, and he laid hands on all who were sick. Many recovered, healed by the sign of the cross.

Not surprisingly, Roch himself came down with the plague, and, rather than burden others, he crawled into a forest hut outside of a village named Piacenza and prepared to die. (Legend says that a spring miraculously appeared, which kept him alive.) One day he looked up and saw a dog trotting toward his hut, bearing a loaf of bread. He approached Roch and laid the bread gently on his chest, then sat down to watch Roch eat. Roch was amazed. The next day the same dog appeared, again with a loaf for Roch. This pattern continued, and the dog also began to nestle next to Roch and lick his wounds. The dog's nobleman owner, Gothard Palastrelli, noticed his dog's behavior, and his curiosity led him to Roch. Impressed by the sick man and his condition, Palastrelli befriended him, and Roch recovered.

Back in France, there was a civil war going on. Roch left for Montpellier accompanied by the faithful dog. But due to Roch's long illness, he was emaciated, and no one recognized him. Roch refused to identify himself as royalty, so he was deemed a spy. He and the dog were thrown in prison. Roch spent the next five years helping fellow prisoners until he succumbed at the age of thirty-two. (At the moment of death, his frightened jailer described the cell as lighted all in blue.) After his death, documents in his possession revealed his true identity.

It is believed that at some point, an angel brought a table into Roch's prison cell, and the message written in gold on the table promised that whoever called upon St. Roch would be free of all contagious diseases. Some sources say that an angel ministered to Roch throughout the last difficult years of his confinement.

Numerous miracles, especially those related to the plague and epidemics, were later attributed to Roch, who was canonized in 1427 and named Patron of Dogs and Dog Lovers, among other titles. His feast day is August 16th, and he is still invoked by Christians against infectious diseases. There are at least twenty churches named after St. Roch in the United States.

So if you come across a statue or an artistic rendition of Roch, you'll know who he was. No more has been learned about the dog, but he appears to have been a brown and white spaniel, often depicted carrying a bread bun in his mouth, faithful to his mission.

FOR THE LOVE OF DOGS

Dear God, please send me someone who'll care!
I'm tired of running, I'm sick with despair.
My body is aching, it's so racked with pain,
and dear God I pray, as I run in the rain.
That someone will love me and give me a home,
a warm cozy bed and a big juicy bone

—Unknown

❦

For the past twenty years I have been in touch with JoAnn Cayce, of Cayce Charities in Thornton, Arkansas. JoAnn and her family and many "earth angels" voluntarily care for the people who live in this small, poverty-stricken town; JoAnn is often referred to as "The Mother Teresa of Southern Arkansas." As she makes her rounds, she often comes in contact with stray dogs and has been bitten several times. She (generously) insists that it's not the dogs' fault. "If you were hungry and no one loved you, you might strike out too." But now she carries a bag of dog food in her truck, to feed any abandoned mutts that approach her along the roads.

Despite the human misery she deals with, JoAnn attempts to make the dogs' lives better too, for they can keep children warm when the gas has been turned off or act as guardians if criminals attempt to break into a house (one wonders what they would steal). And for children who have few toys or ways to pass the time, a dog can be a welcome and loving companion.

Often, JoAnn says, people there don't know how to take care of a dog, and with a bit of encouragement, the dog's situation can be improved. On one occasion, "I had gone by and watched a certain dog freeze in an old doghouse for about three weeks," she says. "One day I went up in the alley to feed the homeless, and as I went by that dog, I said, 'Dog, I don't know your name but before I go to bed tonight, I am going to see that you are out of that mud hole and in a warm place to sleep, or I will not go to bed.'

"I did not get up there until about nine or ten that night, but that dog was waiting as if he understood the promise. He was standing up in the mud, waiting. When I left, he was full and huddling in the warmth of not only insulation—straw, leaves, and hay—but he had felt the pats of love and words. I feel he will remember the visit a long time.

"In fact, I told the owner how much her dog deserved a better place, and if he could bark and scare danger away and be such a friend to her, the least she could do was get him a pan to eat out of instead of off the muddy ground. Surely she could move his house to a dry place, and pat and talk to him some each day. . . . She seemed to look at the dog with some respect in the lights of my truck as I left. She may have just really seen that dog for the first time

"I did notice today that he has a pan out! He doesn't seem to be hunting something around his house. Makes me think his stomach is acquainted with something besides air.

"Oh, to care, to care—it feels so good."[4]

PAW IT FORWARD

Blessed is the person who has earned the love of an old dog.

—SIDNEY JEANNE SEWARD

When Libby Cascaden saw her coworker's litter of red chow-mix puppies, she melted. *Of course* her daughter and son could have one! The Cascadens chose Sam, a lively little pup with long red hair and a black tongue who seemed as happy with the transaction as the family was. "He loved to lick the children's faces, to run with them, and to sleep curled up beside my son," says Libby.

Everything was fine at first. However, as Sam grew, he needed to go out more frequently for exercise, and Libby's children were too small to walk and control him by themselves. Worse, Sam had quickly figured out how to dig underneath their fence and escape. Libby and the children would scour the neighborhood looking for their adventurous pup, or a kind neighbor would call the phone number on Sam's collar or bring him home.

Libby's schedule had not expanded to cover these frequent forays, and the children were not learning about responsibility as she had envisioned. In fact, she was having major second thoughts about caring for a dog, *any* dog. One evening she had a talk with the kids. "Maybe it would be better if Grandma and Grandpa took Sam to their house," she suggested. The kids were fine with the arrangements—after all, Grandma and Grandpa lived right next door!

Thus, for the next thirteen years, Sam was both an inside and outside pet. He slept anywhere that was convenient, but his favorite spot was outside, near the floor furnace under Grandma and Grandpa's house. He enjoyed everyone in the family but his favorite was Grandpa, "Pa" as everyone called him. Sam, all sixty pounds of him, would crawl up into Pa's lap as he sat in the den in his favorite chair. Day in and day out, he greeted Pa with enthusiasm and sat by his side, comforting him as Pa's good health slipped away.

The day that Pa died, Sam took one of Pa's slippers to his nest under the house and refused to emerge. When his grieving eventually ended, he began to care for Ma in the same loyal way.

Eventually Sam grew old and was plagued by arthritis. When spring arrived, Ma made an appointment for Sam at the vet's. His long red coat needed grooming, and he'd probably feel better if he had a "spring cleaning" bath too. Ma was concerned, however, about whether Sam could get into the car by himself, for there were many times now when even climbing the three porch steps seemed to be too much for him. "Ma was so nervous about lifting Sam that she worried about it all night," Libby recalls. "She was sure it was not going to be possible." The next morning Libby went over to calm her down and lend a hand.

Sam gave it a valiant effort. He had not ridden in the car recently, but once he knew what was expected of him, he tried to get into the back seat. Instead, he stumbled. He just didn't have the strength or energy to lift his rotund frame onto the back seat.

Libby attempted to lift Sam's front paws to help him into the car, but he gently nipped at her to let her know that the pain was too great. Instead, he sat wearily at the open car door for a few minutes, temporarily defeated but gathering his strength. Rallying a little, he then hobbled around the yard on his leash, working the kinks out of his arthritic legs.

Suddenly and seemingly out of nowhere, an unaccompanied boxer dog appeared on the sidewalk directly in front of Ma's house. He was large, gray, and intimidating and was headed directly toward Sam. Dogs rarely walk around the neighborhood unleashed, and Libby had never seen this one before. Sam was so vulnerable . . . "Sam!" Ma screamed, anticipating a lunge from the stray.

But the boxer did not attack. Instead he cautiously approached Sam, who gave the obligatory low, warning growl, and they sniffed each other and circled as Libby tried to pull Sam back. "Sam may be old but he still thinks he is the alpha male, at least around these parts," Libby says. "I could tell by the way that the hair stood up on his back that he wanted to assert his dominance, but old age and perhaps wisdom kept him from doing so."

Then an unexpected thing happened.

The strange dog trotted over to Ma's car, where both back doors still stood open. Briskly he jumped up into the back seat, wiggled around to make himself comfortable, and lay down for a few seconds. He and Sam exchanged looks, and then the visitor stood up and gracefully exited through the other door. Within moments he was gone.

The women were speechless. What had the dogs been saying to each other? Was the boxer teasing Sam? "Hey, old guy! Here's the way you do it!" Or was he cheering Sam on? "C'mon, fella—just one more try!"

Apparently Sam would not be outdone by a young whippersnapper. "When the gray dog disappeared, Sam hobbled his way over to the car at a turtle's pace—but he was moving!—and put his front paws up into the seat," says Libby. "I lifted his hefty bottom, and we all pushed as he finally climbed in."

What an ordeal. "The whole thing left Ma shaking in her loafers, and I'm pretty sure she had to take a tranquilizer at home," says Libby. But Sam got to the vet, and he got his bath and a shave and a lot of pampering and seemed very happy when Ma picked him up that afternoon.

Later, as her now-grown children fussed over him, Libby felt the tears gathering. This might well be Sam's final summer. But she knew his would not be a lonely leave-taking. At least one friend was waiting to show him the ropes.

Guardian in Their Midst

❧

I was a guest on KLIF radio in Dallas. A caller told us that he had been part of a recent search for a lost teenager. "The only reason we found her," he said, "was that we kept following the sound of a dog constantly barking."

"Her dog?" I asked.

"She didn't have one," he answered. "The barking stopped just as we came upon her, but no one ever saw a dog."

Guardian angel in disguise? Or maybe a real dog acting like an earth angel? It happens.

❧

Rusty was the first puppy Diana and Ernest Bensch owned, a sweet little Queensland heeler with a laid-back attitude. Diana had not been all that enthused about adopting a dog, but when their daughter was born in 2007, she realized that having pets would be a real advantage for Victoria. The Bensches, along with various family members, live outside the small town of Cordes Lake, Arizona, about thirty miles east of Prescott. The terrain is mostly desert, with a lot of brush, cactus, and smaller trees surrounding their sprawling eighty-acre ranch. There are no other children around, so from the first, Rusty became little Victoria's companion. (Not to mention the two horses, Trooper and Chex, ten or fifteen head of cattle, and various other species.) Rusty was also in charge of chasing off the occasional coyote or wild pig that invaded the area, and she worked at it faithfully. Eventually a friend unexpectedly presented the family with another Queensland heeler named Blue. "Rusty needs a partner," the friend observed, and the Bensches okayed the plan.

However, if Rusty was mellow, Blue was anything but. Active and feisty, older than a puppy but not quite an adult, Blue didn't seem to know where he fit. He did learn to play "fetch," and soon toddler Victoria was throwing the ball for him, squealing in delight when he brought it back to her. However, things were done on Blue's timetable, and if he had another plan, nothing got in his way, not even Victoria. Often he'd spy a rabbit and take off after it in the middle of a game, leaving her and Rusty behind. Queensland heelers, intelligent and aware, are usually very loyal to their owners. Willful Blue didn't seem to fit the pattern.

The Bensches' ranch is completely fenced, with two outbuildings, some unused trailers, and several vehicles. It abuts open government land. Victoria has a fenced play area, including a swing set, near the house. During this past Christmas season, Santa had brought her a trampoline to use in that area. The little girl had figured out how to entice Blue onto the trampoline, and so the two of them now spent many hours bouncing off their energy. The trampoline also encouraged Victoria to play near the house. She and her parents often walked the acreage, but she had been cautioned many times never to explore by herself. Her dad acknowledges that Victoria "is headstrong and adventuresome." But she is usually obedient too (her aunt Kimberly calls her the family's little angel). And that's why, when three-year-old Victoria vanished on Thursday, February 22, 2010, her parents didn't initially believe that she would have gone into the remote and rocky woods alone.

"It was an ordinary day," Diana recalls. "We had purchased a bunk bed for Victoria, which had been delivered and set up that morning, and she was very excited about having a bed with stairs." Diana had made up the bed, and she didn't want Victoria to play on it yet. Time for some outdoor exercise, she decided. Mom, daughter, and the two dogs went outside, and Victoria started to jump on the trampoline. It was about 4:30 on a warm and sunny afternoon, and Diana started thinking about planting the garden. What seeds should they start? At this point, she realized she needed to make a quick trip inside. "I'll be right back," she told Victoria, who was still bouncing, and hurried in. In a moment or two, she was back, talking on her cell phone to Ernest, who had called to let her know he was on his way home from work. Diana scanned the backyard and immediately noticed that her daughter was gone. "Ernest," she cried out, "Victoria's not here!"

"What?"

"She's not in the yard!"

"I'll be home in about five minutes," Ernest reassured her. Diana started to run, calling her daughter's name. It was then that she noticed Blue was missing too. "I was freaking out," Diana says. "I had just seen her. How could she be gone?"

She kept calling, and when Ernest sped into the driveway, he joined her. "As we searched, I thought of every possibility," she says. Had the three-year-old tumbled down a ravine? Was she injured somewhere and unable to respond? Worse, had someone snatched her? Given the fence around their property, that was highly unlikely, but still . . . They searched the outbuildings, and even the horse corral. Victoria had already sat on a horse but was not yet ready to ride—would she have attempted something like that by herself? The area was so vast. At about six p.m. Diana, now in a state of terror, phoned the Yavapai County Sheriff's Office. The family's nightmare had begun.

Law personnel take a missing child very seriously. Many of them, of course, are parents, and can identify with a distraught mother or father. But they must also remain as detached as possible while investigating. The first officer to arrive at the ranch declared the house a possible crime scene and told Ernest and Diana that, not only could they not enter their home, but they also could not leave the property to search for their child. (In case of a kidnapping, one of them would have to be there to receive a call.) A police officer was stationed in the yard, where he would remain until the next day. As the word spread, despite the setting sun, searchers assembled at the sheriff's office, along with their all-terrain vehicles, high-powered lights, and tracking dogs. Some came on horseback. The sheriff deputies set up roadblocks where they grimly flagged down cars and popped trunks. "She's wearing a brown T-shirt and pink pants . . . only three years old . . ." The details were circulated, but there were no answers. As darkness set in and many searchers temporarily suspended their efforts, deputies visited every registered sex offender in the area. All were cooperative, and nothing suspicious was found.

Diana had called her sister in Florida "to keep me from losing it," and the police were sensitive as they continued to ask questions of her. Relatives were arriving, and around midnight, the house ban was lifted. Someone called the media so Diana could plead for her daughter's return, should the police allow her to do so.

"There was a report of a child in a Family Dollar Store in Phoenix who looked like Victoria, but it didn't pan out," Diana says. By now she was pacing the floor, watching the TV for any news, and praying. Nighttime temperatures in February usually sank to thirty degrees or below, and Victoria had not been wearing a coat. How could she stay warm? There were predators in those mountains too, including bobcats and wolves. A little child would be no match for them.

And where was Blue? He had disappeared at the same time, but was he with Victoria? "Would he stay with your daughter and try to protect her?" a police officer asked. Given his lack of loyalty, Diana had to say no. If Blue saw something more interesting than Victoria, he would have been off like a shot. What if Victoria had been abducted and Blue had been killed? Kim and her husband stayed with Diana but tried not to speak of what was on everyone's mind.

By the time the sun rose, at least sixty search-and-rescue volunteers had gathered, but their fervor was flagging. The little girl had been missing for fifteen hours by then, and if she had spent that time in the freezing cold, the outcome was probably not going to be a good one. It had been a tough night for Ernest too, but now his search ban was lifted. "I'm going!" he told Diana and sped to join the others.

Now, with the dawn, they could use helicopters. One of the paramedics climbed into a Department of Public Safety plane. He felt strongly that Victoria was nearby. She was small, and darkness had come quickly after she was reported missing. She would not have had time to travel very far from her home. Not fifteen minutes into the air, the paramedic squinted down at a dry ravine about three-quarters of a mile from the ranch—and thought he saw movement. Yes! He alerted his partner. Wasn't that a dog?

It was a blue-gray dog, the color of Blue. He had been moving around but peered upward as the helicopter approached. The men looked for a place to land on the rough vegetation, and it was then that they spotted Victoria. She was lying face down in the ravine, motionless. If it wasn't for Blue's activity, they might not have seen her.

Quickly the plane landed, and the men approached the little bundle on the ground. Then suddenly, she moved! Relief washed over the men, as Victoria turned over and saw them.

She was dirty, with tangled hair and scratches on her face. Her cheeks were smudged with tears, and she was barefoot. But she was alive! The paramedic started toward her, but Blue was not happy about it. He trotted back and forth in front of Victoria, growling and agitated, not at all sure whether anyone should get close.

Slowly, the paramedic walked toward Victoria, hoping to avoid getting attacked by Blue. He knelt down next to her. "I'm going to take you to your Mommy." Her face lighted up in a smile, and she lifted her arms. At that point, Blue's entire demeanor changed. His body relaxed, his tail began to wag, and he scampered around almost playfully as the men attended to Victoria. When it was time to go, he jumped eagerly into the helicopter after her.

It seemed as if the entire town had turned out to welcome Victoria. People were hugging one another, cheering, and waving as the chopper landed at the command post to pick up Diana. The joy had not set in as yet, for she was still stunned. Despite all odds, her daughter was alive! Blue leaped out of the helicopter to greet her but ran back to Victoria once he realized she was still on the plane. He seemed a bit confused, and a bystander took charge of him so mother and daughter could reunite with tearful hugs.

The doctors at Phoenix Children's Hospital told Diana that Victoria was extremely lucky to have survived the frigid night with only swollen feet and possible frostbite, especially since she had taken off her shoes, which kept slipping on the rough terrain. The damage could have been much worse. As the story unfolded, it was obvious that Blue had saved Victoria's life. Instead of running off on his own pursuits, he apparently recognized the danger she was facing, and he had lain next to her the entire night, shielding her from predators and cold, just as he would have done for any member of the pack. Blue had grown up at last.

But why had Victoria left home in the first place? As she tried to explain at the hospital, she'd simply been looking for Rusty (who had actually been on the porch the entire time). But when Blue saw Victoria wandering off, he followed her. "I don't think she thought she had done anything wrong," says her aunt Kimberly. "She probably just got turned around. It's easy to do." But darkness fell quickly, and the toddler was hopelessly lost.

"I looked at the moon all night," she told her family. So far it's the only thing she remembers.

Her parents, of course, lived a lifetime in those terrible fifteen hours. "The things I thought were important before— not important," says Diana. "She's the most important thing to me." Diana is still sleeping in Victoria's room, and she isn't sure when she'll stop. Ernest chokes up each time he praises the rescue teams. Neither can find words to express their gratitude to the hundreds of people, mostly strangers, who put someone's emergency ahead of their own convenience and made a miracle. Even a dog food company has expressed its pleasure in the outcome by giving Blue free dog food for the rest of his life. Its name? Blue Buffalo Pet Food Company.

But on the night of the rescue, Blue had his very own steak. It was a small enough gift for the guardian in their midst.

THE PASTOR'S PAL

N. (name of animal) may you be blessed in the Name of the Father, and of the Son and of the Holy Spirit. May you and N. (the name of the owner) enjoy life together and find joy with the God who created you.

—BLESSING OF THE PETS

⚜

One of life's pleasures that Catholic priests (and perhaps clergy of other faiths) usually relinquish is pet ownership. Oh, there are rectories that boast beautiful fish tanks, but can they really substitute for a relationship with man's best friend? Parish life can be lonely, and a dog (sometimes a cat, depending on the cat) can offer much-needed companionship. So says the Reverend Donald Buhr, pastor of Our Lady of the Holy

Cross Catholic Church, in the St. Louis, Missouri, diocese. His Lab and border collie mix, Elijah, is the only dog he knows who attends daily mass.

Animals in church? It sounds vaguely disrespectful, tolerance carried too far. But pets do have a place in parish life. The Blessings of the Animals Feast is usually celebrated in honor of St. Francis sometime in October, when owners (mainly children) bring their pets to church for personal blessings. And some (mostly Protestant) churches around the country are experimenting with pet liturgies; in honor of National Dog Week in 2010, Calvary Episcopal Church in Danvers, Massachusetts, sponsored the Perfect Paws Pet Ministry, which attracted over one hundred dogs and their owners.

So far, the votes are not in. Animals have been known to fight or disrupt a service. One minister recalls a time when several dogs howled their way through the featured hymn, "All Creatures of Our God and King." At another service, one canine became so rambunctious that its owner quickly took him outside, "just like an unruly child," the owner pointed out.

Father Buhr has always been a dog lover, but he didn't feel that pets fit into the lifestyle of a priest. "It doesn't sound right and doesn't seem right," he says. Nine years ago, however, when Father was associate pastor at St. John the Baptist Catholic Church, he decided to give it a try. His church was in a rural area, where a dog would be able to run free in the fields and forests and have little involvement with people. He had heard that border collies were the smartest breed and black Labs the gentlest, but how would he find this perfect mix?

"The very next day I saw an ad in the paper," Father says. "A guy was moving and had to get rid of his dog—a one-year-old border collie and black Lab mix." Interestingly, the slim black dog had white fur on his chest in the shape of a cross. (Does this remind you of St. Roch?) The whole thing seemed heaven sent, Father decided, and he brought the dog home, naming him Elijah, "because he came into my life like a whirlwind, the same way Elijah went up to heaven."

While at St. John the Baptist, Elijah never entered the church itself. But in summer 2009, the sixty-nine-year-old priest was named pastor at Our Lady of the Holy Cross Catholic Church, an inner-city parish in St. Louis. The gothic church is stunningly beautiful, with stained glass windows twenty-five feet high and a spire that's visible for miles. The processional cross bears the crucified Christ as an African American. But church enrollment is small, about 200 families, and the neighborhood is busy. Although there's a chain-link fence around the big backyard, Father knew he would have to keep close tabs on Elijah. The dog would no doubt get into the church on occasion, and what if he made a nuisance of himself? Father Don took it to the parishioners as soon as he arrived. "If for any reason Elijah distracts you, please let me know," he told them. "I don't want anyone's prayers to be disturbed."

The congregation was willing to take a chance on letting a dog attend Mass, and during the next few weeks, they got to know the new arrival. Elijah settled in and learned the ropes of being a "church dog" (as named by the children). He familiarized himself with the kneelers, the altar, and on colder days, a spot near the radiator (where he sometimes curls up for a nap).

Parishioners noted that Elijah was somewhat noisy outside; he still barks continuously at squirrels although he's never caught one ("he lives in hope," Father says). But Elijah has never made a sound inside the church.

What are the official duties of a church dog? Now a pro, at a typical Mass Elijah may wander down the aisle and check the pews, looking for a pat or a hug. Or stroll onto the altar to sit next to Father Buhr or an acolyte (who might stroke Elijah with one hand while ringing the bells with the other). And when people line up to receive Holy Communion, Elijah goes to his regular place in front of the first pew on the left, watching intently but reverently as Father distributes the Eucharist. People step around him with no problem. Why does he choose that same spot each day? Could he be seeing angels? Who knows? There is little research available on church dogs.

At the end of Mass, Elijah takes his place in front of the servers, deacons, and priest and leads them down the main aisle. He is now so much a part of everything that it's rare for someone to be startled at his inclusion. Father knew that his dog was wholeheartedly accepted when a parishioner left a photograph of priest and pup in the parish office with a hand-written caption: "Our leader, shown along with Father Don."

Father hopes that his parish's wholehearted acceptance of Elijah might attract other dog lovers, folks who haven't been to church in a while and would like to meet Elijah. More than one pet lover has asked if he might bring his dog to church, too, but Father says no. Two or more animals together might incite a riot. Leaving well enough alone seems the best course.

"Isn't it clever on God's part that he can use something as ordinary as a dog to spread his message?" Father points out. "He's got to be laughing at the whole thing."

SNOW ANGEL

They say that every dog lover has one dog in their life that is their soul mate, the one with whom they share a wondrous and unexplainable connection.

—LINDA BAXTER

᳇

"Looks like a major snowstorm is heading our way, folks," announced the radio weatherman. Linda Baxter paused momentarily while buttoning her coat and peered out the window of her Marion, Indiana, home. Yes, she could see a few flakes already swirling in what appeared to be a rising wind. How fortunate that her seven-year-old son Michael had already boarded his school bus, and kindergartner Lesley's school was only a block and a half away, if they left by the back gate.

Fleetingly, Linda wondered why classes hadn't been cancelled already—Indiana storms could get quite heavy in a brief amount of time. But she pushed the worry out of her mind as she reached for her keys and directed Lesley onto the back porch. "Wait for Mommy, honey," she called over her shoulder, as she locked the door and caught up to Lesley.

Linda enjoyed walking her daughter to and from school each day. It was an easy route, great exercise for Linda's degenerative arthritis, and a chance for them to talk quietly one-on-one. Lesley enjoyed their routine, too, because it meant that she could stop to pat her best friend, Punkie, the handsome German shepherd who lived next door. Punkie's owners, the Roths, were an older couple who had moved in about a year ago. Punkie was Erv Roth's constant companion ("joined at the hip" was the way Jane Roth put it), and because Erv liked to tinker in his garage, it was just a matter of time before Michael and Lesley had met him and fallen in love with Punkie too.

"Somehow our families blended," says Linda. "One of the kids' favorite things to do was to swing with Jane, Erv, and Punkie on the front porch. Michael's favorite game was to shovel Erv's walk and not get caught. One Mother's Day we snuck over during the night and planted flowers in Jane's flower barrel."

Each day since the beginning of school, Lesley had been telling Punkie all about kindergarten, as well as her special secrets. The large black and tan dog would listen patiently, then give Lesley a sloppy kiss to show she understood. However, as the days grew colder, the Roths were keeping Punkie inside most of the time. "I miss Punkie, Mom," Lesley said as they passed the empty yard.

"I do too," Linda agreed. "But you want Punkie to be safe and warm inside, don't you?"

Lesley nodded. It was almost too cold to talk. Flakes were coming down in full force, and the wind had picked up. Quickly Linda brought Lesley to her classroom, gave her a goodbye hug, and hurried home. The snow was already a few inches deep.

By midmorning, the announcements of school closings were all over the TV news. "Blizzard conditions are predicted," warned the forecasters. There was the chance of whiteouts, those situations in which the falling snow became so dense that a person would lose perspective and sense of direction. *At least*

I don't have to drive, Linda thought as she bundled up again. That would certainly be dangerous. Lesley's school was letting out early, and with any luck, they'd be safely home in a matter of minutes. Hopefully, Michael's bus would be a little late. Linda left the front door open, but she knew Michael would worry if she was not at home when he arrived. This day was becoming so complicated!

When Linda stepped out the back door for the noon hike to school, the snow was already up to her knees. None of the neighbors had shoveled yet, knowing that the wind would simply whip the drifts back onto their sidewalks. This made walking almost impossible. For the first time, Linda was afraid. How was her small daughter going to cope with the deepening snow? How she envied Punkie, as she passed the Roths' house and pictured the dog lying on a warm rug near Erv's chair. And there was no one she could call on for help—their street was populated mostly by retired couples such as the Roths. It was up to her to protect her children.

Staggering into the school, her back aching from the effort, Linda went to the kindergarten room and helped the teacher bundle the last few children into their coats. Then she took

Lesley's hand and started out again, pushing the outer door hard to get it open. The school was nearly deserted.

"When we stepped outside, the wind stole Lesley's breath and nearly lifted her off her feet," Linda says. "She clung to my hand, and I tried my best to shield her, but the snow had drifted so high she could hardly walk." Each step was a battle, and within minutes Lesley was wet, exhausted, and in tears. "Come on, honey, just a little bit farther." Linda tried to encourage her, but it was almost hopeless. Lesley was too short to make headway through the mounting drifts and too heavy for Linda to carry.

The snow swirled around them, hitting their faces with needlelike flakes. "Our fingers and feet were numb, our chests ached, and our cheeks were wind burnt," Linda says. The harsh wind bit at their noses, and the wetter they were, the more painful each breath became. Linda dragged Lesley on, a few inches at a time, but finally Lesley collapsed into a snow bank and Linda fell alongside her, her back burning with pain. They lay for a moment, exhausted and spent, then Linda struggled to her feet again. She knew it was dangerous to lie down in the snow; people fell asleep and froze to death that way. They had to keep going. Reaching for her daughter, Linda looked up at the sky, and suddenly she was terrified.

In the few moments they had taken to rest, the storm had intensified. The snow was so thick now that it was blotting out the items around them, even the trees and houses, and Linda was completely disoriented. The dreaded whiteout. "I couldn't tell which direction we were facing or where we were. I was afraid to move because if I went the wrong way we could be in the street, and any oncoming traffic would never see us." People died under those conditions too. What should they do? What *could* they do?

They could pray. They could ask the God who made the snow to deliver them out of it. Linda gathered Lesley into her arms and, still lying in the drift, they prayed. "Dear Lord, help us to find our way home." Then Linda pulled her exhausted daughter to her feet. With the last of their strength, they had to try again.

Just then, Linda spotted a dark shape just ahead—a large bush, a trash can? No, this shape was moving. "Out of the blinding snow came an angel sent by God to help us," Linda says. It was Punkie! The dog ran straight to Lesley and gave her a wet kiss.

"Punkie!" Lesley cried in delight. "Take us home!" She grabbed hold of Punkie's collar with one hand and tightened her grasp on Linda with the other. As if she understood everything, Punkie began to lead them in a specific direction, fighting her way through huge drifts.

But Linda wondered how Punkie would know the right path. Even a dog with a fine sense of smell was at a disadvantage in this terrible weather. But Punkie seemed to know exactly what she was doing. She leaped forward again and again, scrambling over the snow banks, dragging Lesley with her. Each step was a struggle, but Punkie wouldn't let them stop. When Lesley occasionally lost her hold on the dog, Punkie would stop and bark to get them going again. "She seemed to realize how dangerous it was for us to be out in the storm, and she kept urging us on." The journey seemed endless, and Linda had lost all track of time and location when suddenly a familiar shape loomed ahead. Her backyard gate! Punkie had brought them safely home.

"Oh, Punkie, thank you! Thank you!" Lesley gasped. She gave the dog a final hug, and then Punkie turned away. As quickly and mysteriously as she had appeared, the dog was gone.

Linda and Lesley struggled through their backyard. With frozen fingers, Linda managed to turn the key in the lock and, exhausted, the two fell into the kitchen. Linda looked at the clock. It had taken them over an hour to travel two blocks. They were soaked and freezing, aching in every bone but safe. Lesley would have a warm bath, and they would share cocoa with marshmallows—everything would taste better now, for the rest of their lives. But before another minute passed, Linda had to call Jane Roth and thank her for Punkie's extraordinary help.

"How did you know we were in trouble?" she asked Jane. "Why would you send Punkie out in that storm?"

"I didn't," Jane explained. "Punkie had been sleeping peacefully next to Erv's chair when, suddenly, she leaped up and started to bark. She seemed very agitated and kept jumping around the back door. Erv finally let her out."

Punkie had disappeared into the blizzard as Erv watched, puzzled. What would possess a dog to go out on such a freezing day? And when Punkie didn't return right away, Erv became worried. It was too dangerous to go out and search for her, so he had begun to call her. His voice was becoming strained when, almost an hour later, an exhausted Punkie dragged herself into the yard, walked wearily into the house, and collapsed beside Erv's chair. "She's sleeping soundly," Jane reported. "And now we know why." Punkie would definitely get a special supper that night.

Tears stung Linda's eyes as she hung up the phone—tears of relief and gratitude, but mostly of love. Punkie's love had saved their lives. She would never know how, but that wasn't important.

The Indiana blizzard turned into a state of emergency, with factories, offices, and schools closed for several days. The temperature dipped below zero, and wind gusts caused many cases of frostbite. However, the mood in the Baxter household was definitely upbeat. "How often we come to a place in life when we are unable to see a way 'home' and every turn seems impossible," Linda says. "It is in those moments that we must trust that the Father is in control, that he knows the way, and he will not let us surrender to the 'blizzard' that surrounds us."

Instead he sent a furry four-legged angel to guide them home at last.

Beautiful Brandi

I'm born again, in dog heaven.

—Neil Steinberg, *Chicago Sun-Times*

On June 12, 2006, Lanie Blackmon of Corona, California, kept a promise she had made to her husband, Ron. Brandi, her precious golden retriever, had been battling lymphoma for eight months, and Lani had promised Ron she would have Brandi put down if the dog was not recovering.

In her heart, however, she'd felt certain Brandi would pull through. She and her dog had been friends for over six years, so close that each sometimes knew what the other was thinking. When the terrible diagnosis came, the couple had immediately chosen chemo treatments, despite the expense, and for a while Brandi rallied, playing with the other two goldens in the family and fetching the green Frisbee that was her favorite toy. But soon everything worsened. Brandi came out of remission, her suffering returned, and when Lanie looked into her friend's trusting brown eyes and saw the weak wave of her tail, she knew what she had to do.

That night, as Lanie returned without Brandi, the house seemed emptier than it had ever been. Lanie couldn't stop crying, and she crawled into bed. She was angry at Ron for pushing her into the decision she'd made. She was tormented by sorrow and unable to believe that life would get better someday. She was even feeling guilty. "Years ago my six-month-old daughter died of SIDS," Lanie says. "It was a terrible time, but now I felt I was grieving more for Brandi than I had for my daughter. And how could that be right?"

Ron, worried about her, peeked in. "Have you seen Brandi's Frisbee?" he asked. "I can't seem to find it for the dogs to play with."

Lanie didn't care. What good was the Frisbee if its owner couldn't use it anymore? "Forget about the Frisbee," she told Ron. "Just leave me alone."

Days passed, but the anguish grew more intense. Her heart was truly broken, and she never imagined death would affect her this way. "Just lying in bed and sleeping off and on wasn't doing anything for the pain," Lanie says. So she started taking sleeping pills, two or three a day. Why not? Nothing could be worse than this.

But she couldn't sleep around the clock. And whenever she awakened, the grief was still there, throughout her body, deep into her soul. Lanie hardly ever drank alcohol, but she decided to start. Soon, in addition to the sleeping pills, she was consuming rum. Ron continued to check on her, and he took on the responsibility of caring for the two other family dogs—Lanie couldn't bring herself to be around them—but there wasn't much else he could do. Lanie wanted Brandi, and that could never be.

"For a good month, into July, I was doing the pills and the alcohol," Lanie says. One morning she awakened, crawled out of bed, and stumbled to the window. What kind of day was it going to be? She opened the shade and peered out. Brandi was sitting in the flower garden.

"I closed my eyes and reopened them to make sure I wasn't seeing things," Lanie says.

It was Brandi.

Lanie stared in disbelief. Was this a dream? Then, a soft whispery voice spoke into her left ear. "Mama, please get out of bed. You did what you had to do for me, and I love you. I am very happy here, and you need to be happy for me."

Tears gathered in Lanie's eyes. She must be hallucinating. Or perhaps this was what happened to people who drank too much alcohol. But the golden dog was still in the garden, and the voice had more to say. "Mama, go to the nearest shelter, and they are there waiting for you." Lanie didn't know what the voice meant by that, but before she could ask, it had one more request.

"Mama, close your eyes." Lanie did. "Now open them." Again, she did, but Brandi had disappeared. Instead, in the flower bed lay the green Frisbie that she and Ron hadn't seen since the day Brandi died.

Lanie threw on some clothes and a baseball cap, ignoring her hangover. She knew that her days of pills and alcohol were over. She hopped into her truck. *I am very happy here . . .*

be happy for me. The voice *had* to be Brandi's. And she had brought such a warm, reassuring message. For the first time since Brandi died, Lanie smiled.

The nearest pound was the Corona Animal Shelter. Lanie had never been there and didn't know why she was going, but if this was Brandi's request, she would honor it. A few minutes later, she was walking into the shelter. "Do you have any goldens?" she heard herself ask, even though another dog was the last thing she wanted. It was far too soon.

"Take a look around," the clerk suggested.

Lanie did. Approaching cage 34, she felt the urge to slow down. "I looked in and looking back at me was Brandi."

She almost screamed, but realized just in time that this dog was the image of Brandi, but brand new. Actually the dog was half of a partnership. His sister was sitting right beside him, just as adorable as he was, and by the time Lanie had made arrangements to adopt him, she knew the female would have to come too.

The pair has proven to be devoted to each other, but also headstrong. It's a challenge that Lanie can manage. "I think Brandi knew these two needed me, and that I had enough love for both of them, and that they would keep me busy enough that I wouldn't have time to think so much about her."

Could a simple dog orchestrate such a powerful and loving healing for her owner? Could a missing toy be a signal from beyond? What matters is that Lanie believes and is prepared for those who attribute these happenings to alcohol, mental instability, or a vivid imagination. But it doesn't upset her. She knows Brandi is happy and waits for her in peace.

Puppies, Puppies Everywhere

Does your dog bite?
No, never.
Oww! I thought you said your dog didn't bite!
He doesn't. That's not my dog.

⤞⧐⤝

With everything Chicagoans Heather and Dave Malecek had gone through to get ready for their wedding on June 14, 2008, one could wonder why they adopted a dog just a month before the Big Day. But life's timing isn't always perfect. One day in May, Heather, who already owned a dog, came across an Internet announcement about a shelter in Indiana that was closing down and offering the remaining animals for adoption. Those left would be euthanized within a few days. "They had posted descriptions of the dogs, and I saw one I liked," she says. Dave had never owned a dog, but he liked Heather's and was willing to take in another. So, aware of the grim deadline, the couple drove to Indiana.

The shelter was not a good place, Heather says. The dog that she had originally seen online was obviously so sick that the couple would incur huge veterinarian bills at a time they could least afford them, with no guarantees that the animal could be saved. Several of the remaining dogs seemed just as fragile. Then Heather spotted a small German shepherd-pit bull mix that seemed a bit more animated. "An attendant took her out of her cage, and the dog looked up at us and promptly rolled over on her back," Heather recalls. "That was a sign to me that she had already accepted us." Dave liked her too. They walked the dog around for a while, decided to name it Indi after its original state, and took it home. "I felt that someone had treated this dog very well," Heather observes, "because she was docile and affectionate right away. She was in good physical shape, too, except her belly seemed a little large for the rest of her."

Dave and Heather had already moved some of their furniture and belongings into their new Chicago apartment but were not living there yet. So Dave took the dog to his home in West Dundee, and Heather's parents promised to babysit both dogs while Heather and Dave honeymooned in Europe for two weeks. The dogs would then move with them into their new home.

Things went according to plan, and despite the last-minute wedding preparations, the couple made a vet appointment so Indi could be spayed, as the Indiana shelter had recommended. The vet, however, had an unexpected announcement. One-year-old Indi was already pregnant, he said. He wouldn't hazard a guess as to how far along she was. Surprised, Heather and Dave decided to get a second opinion.

"That vet took an x-ray and told us that Indi wasn't pregnant after all, only going into heat, and sick with kennel cough, an upper respiratory ailment," says Heather. "We assumed he was right, since an x-ray would certainly show whatever was there." False pregnancies were common in some breeds, the vet assured them. Given their packed schedules by now, the couple decided to postpone spaying Indi until they returned.

The wedding day was memorable, and the Maleceks gave Indi a goodbye hug before leaving for the airport. Dave noticed that her belly seemed even larger, but he was no dog expert. Two weeks later, they returned, happy but exhausted. Heather's parents picked them up at the airport.

"How was Indi while we were gone?" Heather asked.

"Well . . ." Heather's mother hesitated. "The dogs got along really well. But Indi's belly is even bigger. I think that first vet was right."

How could that be? Nothing had shown up on the x-ray. But when both of them went to greet Indi, they saw for themselves. Indi was definitely going to be a mother soon. "I think we'd better stay here tonight," Heather suggested. "Just in case."

It was a good decision, for shortly after midnight Heather awakened to see Indi giving birth to two puppies on her parents' white living room rug. She woke everyone, and together they watched as Indi's puppies kept coming. By three a.m., there were thirteen puppies in the living room, an amazing number for such a small dog. Even more unique, there seemed to be two litters involved. (A dog can conceive more puppies when already pregnant, although it is rare.) Indi had handled everything, including cleanup, just the way she was supposed to. But now as she began to feed her brood, Heather and Dave realized that there was a problem: Indi would be able to nurse only eight puppies at a time. Where would she get the stamina—and enough milk—to care for all of them?

Heather had planned to use the summer months to line up a teaching job for fall. Dave was due back at his accounting firm. And of course, they had been looking forward to settling down in their first home, just the two of them and the two dogs. But plans change, and Indi had to be their first priority now. Heather and Dave moved into Heather's parents' home, and as Indi's strength faded, they began to feed milk supplements to the puppies.

Although Dave and Heather's parents helped as much as they could, Heather was the primary caregiver, and her responsibilities never seemed to wane. With each puppy needing nourishment every four hours, she set her alarm and slept only briefly between feedings. (The larger pups from one litter ate quickly, but the smaller puppies took at least twenty minutes each to feed.) Heather regulated a heating lamp (later a space heater) to keep them warm, cleaned their cages, clipped their nails, and bathed each one two or three times a week. She also read up on questions such as: When do their eyes open? When is it safe to bring them outside? When do they begin eating solid food? Despite her fatigue and the unexpected expenses involved, she was falling in love with her tiny charges, and her mission was to rescue them all.

"It was kind of bad timing," Heather admits. "We were looking forward to relaxing, because the year leading up to a wedding can be stressful. But there was no rest for the weary." Heather also spent time meeting potential adoptees. Word had spread quickly. "I had to make sure each one would go to a good home," she says. "Of course I didn't want any of them to leave, but it had to be done."

Finally, the long summer faded, and on August 19, after many interviews, the first two puppies moved to permanent homes. The others followed gradually. All of the puppies were in robust health, and Heather had made friends with the adopting families, which took some of the sting out of separating. But at the end, Heather and Dave decided to keep the last puppy, as a connection to the others.

All three dogs now live with Heather and Dave in Chicago, and yes, the couple is often teased about being well prepared for parenthood due to their adventure with the pups. But despite the extra work complicating their wedding plans, they would do it again without a qualm.

⚮

Barbara Thill is the mother of fourteen children. Although they are all grown now, there was a time when sixteen people actually lived together in their modest home in suburban Chicago. Correction: sixteen people and a dog. The second-oldest Thill son had not wanted his siblings to grow up without a dog, so he brought one home right after his high school graduation, and it turned out to be an excellent decision. "Cinnamon was a golden retriever and very good with the children," Barbara says. "She never snapped at anyone and was very obedient. Since she was also easy to train, the kids taught her how to jump to close the kitchen door, as well as to sit and roll over."

Inevitably with all that foot traffic, the family's backyard gate was left open one day, and Cinnamon experienced freedom for the first time. She met the black Lab at the end of the block and as they say, the rest was history.

When Cinnamon delivered, however, the family was in shock. Thoughtfully, their dog had delivered fourteen puppies. Fourteen. "One for each of us!" the kids chorused.

There was no way the family was going to keep fourteen dogs. But as Barbara checked the litter, she decided not to say anything immediately. The children could learn a lot about life and death and responsibility by helping Cinnamon care for the puppies. Instead of arguing, the kids found a box and some towels to keep the newborns warm. It was then that Barbara discovered that one of the pups was stillborn. A second died two days later. The children mourned, but there were still twelve puppies for them to watch over. Twelve.

By the time the pups were six weeks old, the house was extremely crowded with puppy paraphernalia and the children admitted they needed new homes. But how to locate twelve willing families? Barbara had noticed that—at least to her—one of the puppies wasn't as cute as the others. That gave her an idea. "We put collars and ribbons on them and ran an ad in the local newspaper," she said. "Hoping to speed things up, we set the sale price at just ten dollars per dog." The ad read, "For Sale—Eleven beautiful puppies and one ugly one."

The phone began to ring. Every caller asked the same question: "How ugly is the ugly dog?"

It was hard to describe puppies over the phone. "Come and see for yourself," Barbara told the first caller, a middle-aged woman. She arrived shortly, looked over the litter, and zeroed in on a particular puppy almost immediately. "I don't think he's *that* ugly," she told Barbara, as she paid her ten dollars.

The kids were watching. "Mom," one whispered, "that's not the ugly puppy—"

"Shhhh," said Barbara. A young couple was approaching, with a child dancing excitedly. The father reached for the chubbiest of the puppies. "It's obvious that he's ugly," he told Barbara defensively, "but we'll love him anyway."

"But . . ." A Thill child began to object, but Barbara sent him in for a nap.

By the end of the weekend, a new lock had been put on the back gate, and Cinnamon was, once again, the only canine in the house.

But, as everyone seemed to notice, a large collection of puppies had moved into the neighborhood. All ugly.

Saving Sam

I explained to Saint Peter I'd rather stay here,
Outside the pearly gate.
I won't be a nuisance, I won't even bark,
I'll be very patient and wait.
I'll be here chewing on a celestial bone,
No matter how long you may be.
I'd miss you so much if I went in alone,
It wouldn't be heaven for me.

—Unknown

Today we hear frequently of children being kidnapped. Although the vast majority of such episodes involve custody battles rather than criminal abductors, it can still be a terrifying experience for everyone involved. And although most of these little victims are returned safely to their parents within a few days, there are always a few whose nightmares don't follow that pattern. So it was with Samuel Connelly.

When Sam was two-and-a-half years old, he and his brother Kenny, aged seven, were taken from their babysitter's home in northern California. "My parents were in the midst of getting a divorce but both had equal custody of us, since they hadn't yet figured out a visitation plan," Sam says. "My mother was involved with another man, and my father had been told by family members that she was planning to run away with this man and take us with them." Mr. Connelly was a construction worker and couldn't provide an adequate home on his own for two small boys. But he was afraid of losing them, so one day he asked some of his friends to pick up his sons from the sitter's home and take them out of town, at least until he and his estranged wife could decide the custody issues. Unfortunately, the "friends" had other ideas. They took Sam and Kenny out of state—Sam does not remember why—and it would be more than three years before the boys would see their parents again.

Sam still struggles with areas of his life, dealing with the years he lost. But he does remember some details. He lived in more than one place during those years, apparently shuffled around whenever the police seemed to get too close (occasionally when in a car, he would be told to get down on the floorboards—a sure sign that a police car was passing). But the years he remembers most occurred in a desolate area in Arizona. He and Kenny lived with a couple who had two daughters and a son of their own. Sam didn't get to spend much time with them. Too small to ask meaningful questions, too young to go to school or come in contact with other adults who might have investigated his situation, Sam had no idea that his mother was searching for him throughout the western United States. Instead, he was very much alone. "I was introduced to fear at a young age," Sam says. "The people who took me had strange spiritual beliefs and talked about demons a lot." Sam was also frequently locked out of the house all day to play by himself. "That's probably why I have such a great imagination today. I had to be my own best friend."

But Sam was not always alone. Like many children his age, he had an imaginary companion. "He was a boy, just a little older than I was," Sam recalls. "I had a lot of nightmares during those years. I thought I saw demons, and I would sometimes cry all night." Except when his friend came to visit. Sam cannot remember the boy's name, but he often told Sam stories to comfort him. "To this day I don't know if he was fully imagined, or if he was an angel," Sam says. "But to me, at that age, he was real."

Sam had another consolation, too, a collie dog named Toby. "Toby was a stray that hung around one of the houses we lived in. He was real skinny, so we fed him. He was such a great-mannered dog that I was allowed to keep him. Later, when we moved, Toby went with us."

For Sam, Toby was not just a dog, but a friend. "I talked to him like a little boy would talk to his brother. I joked with him, wrestled with him. He ate my veggies, and I ate a few of his milk bones." Toby served as different characters in Sam's mind. He became a bank robber when Sam played "policeman," a space explorer, a soldier (but that didn't last long, because Toby would fetch the "grenade" and bring it back to Sam!).

When thunderstorms came, he was a gentle father, letting the frightened child cling tightly to him.

The collie was watchful, too. Once Sam was playing on the second floor of an old barn, on the property where he lived, and he was looking out the window, waving at Toby. Suddenly Sam lost his balance and fell out the window. "I didn't really get hurt, just the wind knocked out of me," Sam says. But Toby was distraught. He ran over, dragged Sam to the house, and stayed with him, barking, until an adult finally came.

Toby's biggest contribution to Sam's well-being probably happened one day when Sam was still a preschooler. It was cold, and Sam would probably have preferred to stay indoors, but instead he was sent out, and the door locked as usual. Sam had brought his G. I. Joe and Star Wars action figures outside, and now he looked for a place to play with them. His eye caught the huge field across the road, filled with weeds and foot-high dead grass. He rarely played there (the barn seemed more fun) but now Sam noticed there were gaps in the weeds that might be just right for building miniature fortresses and battlefields. Excited, he gathered his toys and crossed the dirt road.

"For the next few hours I was a four-year-old god, directing a war between Luke Skywalker and the G.I. Joe ground patrol in an intergalactic invasion on earth," Sam says. "I remember running all through the field, as my hero and villain flew through the air shooting missiles at each other. I rolled on the ground, jumping over tiny anthill villages, and crawled through the grass, hidden to the outside world."

Then to his horror, Sam heard a terrifying sound, a high-pitched shriek. It was Toby! He had just been let outside, but instead, he was jumping around, yelping in pain. There seemed to be some kind of silver thing on his leg. "Help Toby! Help Toby!" Screaming, Sam abandoned his toys and ran across the field to his dog. The man who was taking care of him and a friend had heard the dog too and came running out of the house. One removed what was discovered to be a trap, and both men then took Toby to the vet, leaving Sam alone with his grief and fear. *He couldn't lose Toby!* he thought, tears running down his cheeks. The dog was the only bright spot in his life.

When the men came home that evening, they had Toby with them. He had a bandaged leg but was going to be all right.

Weakly, the dog licked Sam's face, and Sam choked back more tears. "What happened to him?" he asked.

"He stepped in a trap," Sam's "guardian" explained. "Looks like there's some in that pasture. You'd better stay out of it."

Sam thought of his toys, still lying where he'd left them when he ran to Toby. He thought about Toby's narrow escape from serious injury. "I decided that I would go out tomorrow morning and get my toys, and then I would never go in the field again," he says. But the next morning, Sam found every one of his action figures in bed with him. "Who brought these in?" he asked at breakfast. No one in the family knew or even seemed to care. A month later, men came to clear and till the pasture across the road, and they found sixty steel-jawed fox traps, all baited, set, and hidden several months ago. Not one had gone off on that fateful day, despite Sam's hours of leaping, running, and jumping throughout the field.

Months passed. By now Sam was old enough to go to school, but he was not enrolled. No one told him why, and he continued his desolate outdoor existence with Toby as his only friend. And then one terrible day, a drunken driver fleeing from the police sped down the dirt road. Toby ran out to bark at the man, but he never slowed down. The man hit Toby and killed him.

Sam cried all night, but there wasn't time for grief. The very next day he and his brother were spirited out of town to another location, and Sam was enrolled in kindergarten. He hardly knew how to relate to the other children in his class, and whenever he thought of Toby, he cried all over again. It's doubtful what kind of adjustment Sam might have made (or not made) in school, but within a few months, his world changed again. "One day some FBI agents and some local police officers came to our school rooms and picked up Kenny and me. They told us we were going to see our mom, but I didn't understand it. I was confused when we were taken to Texas, and then California, and finally to court, and she pulled me to her and kissed my face and cried. She was a stranger to me, and my life made no sense at all."

Sam would like to say that as the years passed, everything worked out, but not everything did. Since he was never allowed to talk about that time, he has only fragmented memories, not always reliable. His mother and father did not seem to know what to do with their rescued sons. "They had gone almost crazy looking for us, but their own lives were so messed up that they hardly knew how to connect with us when we came home." Even today, as a loving husband and father, Sam is still learning about what happened during those difficult years. However, despite them, he realizes that the unseen hand of God never left him. The imaginary friend, protection in the field, and especially Toby—Sam believes they were all consolations sent to help him through.

One aspect in particular still causes him to wonder. How did the FBI finally find them? Sam suspects it may be because of Toby. Because the drunken driver who hit the dog was fleeing from the police, law enforcement came onto the property and obviously became aware of the situation there. Was it only a coincidence that a few months later the FBI visited the site with a warrant, found photographs of the boys, and traced them to their new school?

"I hated the man who killed my dog, but with all the mess that happened over the next few months, the moving and the court appearances, I probably would not have been able to keep Toby," he says. So, in a way, Toby's last act of love and sacrifice led to Sam's freedom. Or perhaps it's even more than that.

"Can a dog actually be an angel in disguise?" Sam asks. "Or are they just heavenly friends that come into our lives at the right time, for the right reason?"

Perhaps someday we'll know.

Prodigal Pup

I talk to him when I'm lonesome like; and I'm sure he
understands.
When he looks at me so attentively, and gently licks my
hands.
Then he rubs his nose on my tailored clothes,
but I never say naught thereat.
For the good Lord knows I can buy more clothes,
But never a friend like that.

—W. Dayton Wedgefarth

In mid-July 2008, twenty-three-year-old Melissa Moeller had a dream about her family's purebred collie. That wasn't unusual—no one had ever forgotten Bo, their first dog. But the memories were tinged with sorrow, because no one had seen him in five years. Bo had disappeared just a few days after the family of eight moved into their home in Northbrook, Illinois, in 2003.

"We'd had Bo for about a year," explains Cheryl, mother of the Moeller clan. "We had adopted him from a collie rescue group in 2002." The dog, friendly and agreeable, had seemed to fit right into the large and bustling family, reminding people of the beautiful and loyal collie in *Lassie Come Home*. But during a busy Memorial Day picnic, Bo disappeared.

The Moeller kids were worried, but somewhat hopeful, too because, along with an implanted ID microchip, Bo also wore a collar with the Moellers' contact information. Surely with all that identification and his beautiful appearance, their collie would be noticed by someone. Melissa led a contingent of siblings and friends who put up posters, searched streets and nearby woods, and canvassed house-to-house; they visited twelve local police stations, along with several shelters. But days turned into weeks and despite their best efforts to publicize his loss, Bo did not come home.

Perhaps the most heartbroken over Bo's loss was then sixteen-year-old Brent Moeller. Brent was Bo's main caretaker and had taught him to sit and roll over, among other tricks. The worst part for Brent was worrying that something bad had happened to Bo. "We didn't understand why the microchip hadn't led us to Bo," says Cheryl, "so we could only wonder if he was even alive." Her husband, Bob, a minister for over thirty years, led prayers every night that someone was taking care of their dog and loving him as much as they did. "There were a lot of tears," Bob remembers. In fact, about a year after the collie disappeared, the local police called Bob because they had found a collie answering Bo's description. "It was a double heartbreak," Bob says, "thinking we had the dog back, but finding out at the police station that it wasn't ours."

Eventually the family got two new dogs, Katie and Rudy. They moved again, this time to Arlington Heights, Illinois. And although they didn't mention Bo very often, none of them forgot him.

So Melissa's dream that July morning was not exactly odd, but there was a new element added. This time Melissa dreamed that Bo had come home, and that the entire family was playing happily with him. "It seemed farfetched," she says, "considering how long he'd been gone," not to mention that Bo wouldn't know where they now lived. So when the family received a call from a shelter in Rockford, Illinois, just a few days later, Bob was afraid to get anyone's hopes up again. "A worker at the shelter told us that the collie they were holding had a microchip with our information on it," Bob says. "Brent and I and two of the girls drove up the next afternoon."

Brent, now twenty-one and out of college, was afraid to hope. Cheryl was afraid for him. "Brent had had some difficult times these past few years. He didn't need another disappointment."

The family entered the facility with hearts pounding. The local news media had been alerted, and a few photographers had stopped by, hoping for a good story. Just then, the back door opened, and a volunteer came in with a large collie on a leash. As the dog approached Brent, he started to whine. It couldn't be. "Bo?" Brent called gently, hardly believing his eyes.

The dog was unkempt and thin but looked to be in good health. Although there were several people in the room by now, he walked directly to Brent. Brent gave a command, and the dog obeyed. Another command and another response; it was Bo! Bob's eyes were wet with tears.

"It was just like old times," Brent says. "He did all the commands I'd taught him like he hadn't missed a day. It was like a Disney movie." His eyes were shining. Along with difficulties, life could bring miracles too. You never knew when one would come along.

The county animal service officer was thrilled as well. This was the first time she had found an animal that had been missing this long. She told the family that a kind resident of Rockford had spotted Bo running loose. He had coaxed Bo into his yard, given him water, and called the shelter. The Moellers had been lucky because if Bo hadn't had a microchip, he would have stayed in the shelter for a week and then would have been put down. A microchip is the size of a grain of rice, and it doesn't hurt an animal to have one put in. Further, it reacts only when a scanner passes over it. In Bo's case, it was worth whatever the cost.

But where had Bo been all this time? Did he walk to the area where he was found, some eighty-five miles north of where the Moellers live? Had a kind family taken care of him, for even part of the time (although he still wore his collar, his city dog tags were gone)? No one will ever know, unless someone comes forward, and so far, that hasn't happened. Shelter personnel suspect that someone had fed Bo, at least occasionally, because he wouldn't have survived for five years without help. He had some hair loss, which can occur when a dog is in the wild, and showed signs of having been caged. But his general health was amazingly good.

As for Melissa, who "couldn't stop smiling and laughing for days" after Bo's return, she hasn't had the dream since and probably won't, now that the real thing is just a few pats away. Bob and Cheryl have agreed to care for Bo until Brent, now living in an apartment, finds a residence that will allow dogs.

And Bo? Like the collie in the book, he obviously never forgot the family who loved him. And his loyalty brought the happy ending everyone sought.[5]

THE LAST ESCORT

We ought to give moral consideration to the welfare of animals . . .
because animals have intrinsic worth. They are creatures of a
Creator who loves them no less than God loves us.

—Valerie Elverton Dixon, *Washington Post*

⟡

Lisa, a flight attendant based in Arizona, met her husband Oscar on a flight, and within two months they were engaged. Oscar was from Antigua, Guatemala, so Lisa was saddened when she realized that most of Oscar's family would not be able to attend their wedding in Phoenix. She had been especially looking forward to meeting his mother, Martita. From what Lisa had heard from Oscar, Martita was an amazing woman. "Tell me about her," Lisa asked, on more than one occasion.

"She mothers everyone," Oscar explained. "Stranger or friend—it makes no difference. Everyone is welcome in her house. Sometimes people stop by just to talk with her. They say it makes them feel better."

A warm person, Lisa surmised.

"And did I mention that she feeds so many needy people that the church has designated her house as a soup kitchen?"

A generous woman, giving and not counting the cost. Lisa was intrigued by Oscar's description. As a new bride, she also felt a bit unsure. She would like to become a person like Martita, to live up to the example she set. But how did one begin?

As time went on, Lisa learned that there was a sort of breech between Oscar and his family in Guatemala. Oscar had been married before, and his divorce had deeply troubled some of his family members, especially his mother. It had happened long before Lisa and Oscar met, and although he and his family seemed to get along better now, there was still occasional tension among them. She and Oscar, and his parents, did eventually visit back and forth, and Lisa felt very relaxed and easy with her father-in-law. With Martita, she was a bit more reserved. "Martita was a truly wonderful woman, in every way," Lisa says. "When we visited Antigua, I would see for myself all the people she helped each day. But I think—because I tended to favor Oscar in whatever family problems existed—I was less involved with her." Thus, when family visits came to an end, Lisa always said good-bye to Martita with a touch of regret. Here had been another opportunity for her to draw closer to her mother-in-law, and she had missed it again.

Then one evening, one of Oscar's sisters phoned. Their mother had died suddenly. Lisa was shocked and sorrowful. Now all she could do was attempt to comfort Oscar. They were on a plane to Guatemala immediately. There again was the unusual scenery, the volcanoes, the age-old architecture and unique street markets, but this time Lisa saw none of the country's beauty. The family mourned together and prepared for tomorrow's funeral.

The next day they sat in the first pew of the old ornate church. Although large, it was almost filled, and there were three priests on the altar. Lisa caught the small sounds of weeping and sighs. She struggled to understand the priest's Spanish as he spoke of Martita. Even he seemed genuinely griefstruck, and Lisa felt as if she wanted to cry too. If only she had been able to really *know* Martita.

Just then Lisa heard light footsteps behind her. She turned slightly and gazed in amazement. A shabby golden-brown dog was coming into the church. "I love animals," Lisa says, "but the church is God's house and a dog doesn't belong in it." Especially an unkempt street dog like that. Surely someone would take it out.

But no one did. The priest went on talking, and the dog walked briskly down the center aisle and sat down in front of the casket, as if she were carrying out an assignment to guard it. Was this some Central American custom? Lisa wondered. For no one was reacting at all. She turned her eyes back to the priest, but it was difficult to concentrate. Why would a stray choose this particular moment to come into church? It was a shame—Martita deserved a dignified farewell, and now this animal had ruined everything. "Someone should catch that dog!" she whispered to Oscar.

"She's not bothering anyone," Oscar said, shrugging.

"Yes, but . . ." Lisa didn't want to argue with her husband, especially on a day like this. Perhaps when everyone left for the cemetery, the dog would go away.

As the service ended, everyone stood to form a procession behind the casket. The dog stood too, and, as if she knew exactly where she was going, trotted in front of everyone else down the center aisle. Lisa grasped Oscar's arm as they walked outside onto the road that led to the cemetery. She had unwisely worn high heels, and her feet were hurting. How was she going to walk on the cobblestone street? One of Oscar's relatives noticed her dilemma. "Would you and Oscar like to ride in the car?"

"I would, thank you." Lisa and Oscar got into the car behind the hearse, and it slowly pulled away. Everyone else followed, walking. Lisa couldn't help it—she looked out the back window. There was the brown dog, marching right behind their car. "It looked as if all the mourners were following the dog," she says. "She seemed to be setting the pace."

When the procession turned into the cemetery, Lisa lost sight of the dog. No doubt she had scampered off somewhere. The car pulled up to the burial site, and as Lisa alighted, she stopped in surprise. Not only was the dog there, but she again had trotted up to the very front, so as not to miss any part of the graveside service.

And she didn't. Oscar's sister gave a eulogy, and he did too, fumbling for a piece of paper on which he had scribbled a final farewell to his mother. Other people spoke. Some wept. Looking around, Lisa realized that many in the large throng were those whom Martita had helped through the years. What a tribute they were paying to her. The dog sat quietly, as if absorbed in it all.

The ceremony ended, and slowly the mourners left, some shaking hands with Lisa, some hugging Oscar as they passed. The dog remained in her place, next to the family; it was almost as if she too were greeting each person. Then, when everyone had gone except the priest and the family, the shabby canine stood, turned, and with deliberate, almost regal steps, marched out of the cemetery—the last guest to leave. Then Lisa realized that, throughout the time she had been with them, the dog had not approached a single person.

The priest watched as the dog disappeared into the busy street market. "That dog has never come into the church before," he commented.

He knew the dog? "Then why did she come to our family's funeral?" Lisa asked.

"She is a stray," the priest explained. "She has no home, no one to belong to. But she was always welcomed at Martita's house."

Martita's house. Lisa thought of the oasis of comfort and calmness her mother-in-law had created. No one had been turned away, not even an insignificant mongrel. Lisa had thought she would never truly know who Martita was. But now she understood. Anyone could be like Martita, if their legacy was love.

BUDDY'S PROMISE

Children and dogs are as necessary to the welfare of the country as Wall Street and the railroads.

—HARRY S. TRUMAN

❧

I met Eric at a church youth group where I spoke about angels. Afterward, he shared his own story with us. It was the first time I had ever thought about the connection between dogs and heaven, and I still can't read about Buddy without getting goose bumps.

When Eric was only a few months old, his family adopted a beagle puppy from a nearby animal shelter. Eric named the dog "Buddy" because that was his first word, even before he learned to say "mama." The two were inseparable. Buddy appointed himself baby Eric's guardian and seemed to know when the little boy needed help, and when he was simply enjoying life. (The two were often the same.)

Buddy was a well-mannered dog, too. The only conflict the family had with him was his behavior late at night. Although Buddy knew that his own bed was in an alcove in the dining room, and that's where he was to stay, he often awakened shortly after midnight and tiptoed (if a dog can tiptoe) up the stairs. Quietly he would enter Eric's bedroom (the door squeaked just a little) and jump up onto Eric's bed. This, of course, immediately awakened the boy. "Buddy would stay at the bottom of the bed," Eric recalls. "He would turn around a few times, to get comfortable, and the bed would shake a little. Then he would lie down with his back snuggled up against my legs and go to sleep. He always kept my legs so warm."

Buddy usually made it back downstairs to his official bed before the family arose, so he could greet each member with innocent brown eyes. But Eric's mother had a certain kind of radar that allowed her to know what was going on without actually seeing it. "Eric, you're going to have to do something about the dog," she would tell her son from time to time. "I don't like animals in people's beds."

"I will," Eric promised. But what, exactly, could he do?

The years passed, Eric's life got busier, and Buddy's slowed down. They still met almost every midnight, but it was becoming harder for Buddy to jump onto the bed. And then one day, Buddy seemed to be in pain. Mom would take him to the vet, she announced at breakfast. Perhaps it was time.

"No!" Eric cried out, embarrassed at the sudden tears flooding his eyes. "Buddy's fine, Mom. Just a little older."

"Eric," his mother said gently. "You know that's not true."

His mother always seemed to know what he was thinking. But life without Buddy? No running in the backyard, no one greeting him each day with joy, no warm back pushed up against his legs at night? Eric thought his heart would break. And when his mother came home from the vet alone, it almost did.

The next days without Buddy were like none Eric had ever known. How could anyone his age feel like the saddest thing in the world had happened? Was this emptiness ever going to end? "The worst part is knowing that I'm never going to see him again," Eric told his mother one evening.

"How do you know that?" his mother asked. "Have you talked to God about it?"

To God? Well, Eric hadn't thought about that. He often prayed, but it was more like a recital of all the things he did that day, his worries, and sometimes his wants. But it couldn't hurt, could it? After all, God was the one who had made Buddy. That night Eric knelt by his bed for a few moments. "God, I need to know something," he began. "Do dogs go to heaven? If they don't, then can we ever see them again? See, I really miss Buddy and the thing is, I'm afraid I'm not going to remember him." His eyes started filling again. That was enough praying for one night.

Eric was in a deep sleep when something awakened him. Had it been the squeak from the door? His parents usually looked in on him on their way to bed. But he didn't hear anything. Then, all of a sudden, he *felt* something at the bottom of the bed—the movement of the mattress, as if someone had jumped on top of it. But there was no one in the room.

Then the hair on Eric's neck stood straight up. The presence at the foot of the bed was moving, turning around as if searching for a comfortable spot, and then lying down against Eric's legs. Eric looked at his alarm clock with its lighted dial. The time was just a few moments after midnight. He looked down at the end of the bed. There was nothing there—yet his legs were as warm as they had ever been, warm right through to his heart.

The next morning Eric's mother noticed a difference in her son. "You must have prayed last night," she said.

"I did, Mom." Eric was still thinking of the presence on his legs. "I think God said that nothing we love ever goes away forever. We keep it alive by remembering. And that's what I'll be doing with Buddy, at least until I learn something more." He grabbed his books and was out the door.

His mother watched him go. That wasn't all that had happened last night, she was sure of it. But mothers try not to interfere with an angel's work. "Thanks, Buddy," she whispered and went to make the coffee.

A HOME FOR MAGGIE

All things bright and beautiful
All creatures great and small,
All things wise and wonderful.
The Lord God made them all.

—CECIL FRANCES ALEXANDER

Tracy Land began working with animals at the Humane Society when she was sixteen, and when she opened her veterinary clinic in 1987 in Cumming, Georgia, she designed it to look homey and welcoming. The cozy front porch with benches, plants, and dormers, and some gingerbread trim—as well as a compassionate staff—all convey the message that here, animals are loved and respected.

That's why, when Dr. Tracy looked at Maggie for the first time, her heart almost broke. A veterinarian sees many abused and neglected animals—it goes with the territory—but some pets just seem more vulnerable than others. Maggie was a black German shepherd, so thin and malnourished that her bones showed through her skin. Covered with open sores from mange and fleas, she was one of ten dogs, all brought into Tracy's clinic, Pet Vet Inc., by the same couple, to be spayed or neutered.

"The leading cause of death among pets today is overpopulation," says Tracy. "Millions of dogs and cats are put down every year because no one wants them." To stem the tide, Tracy devotes a great part of her practice to encouraging early sterilization; she and her partners have done more than 65,000 surgeries since 1997, and at least 10,000 were kittens and puppies just six or seven weeks old. With today's anesthetics, advanced monitoring equipment, and surgical techniques (some of which Tracy has developed and teaches to other vets), "not only are these procedures safe in young animals, the risk of complications and the recovery period are both lower than in mature pets," she says.

"Sadly, it often seems that the people who can least afford them have the most pets," Tracy acknowledges. "In the case of these ten dogs, a Humane Society group was paying for all the spays and neuters. But the owners wanted other care too—vaccinations, wormings, and mange treatment."

Now, as she gently examined the neglected dog, Tracy wondered if it was too late to give Maggie a happy life. The staff got busy cleaning the dogs and preparing them for the procedure. At least they wouldn't give birth to more unwanted puppies.

Recovery typically takes a few hours, and all came through just fine, except for Maggie. She seemed sluggish, and Tracy discovered that she was bleeding into her abdomen. Such things occasionally happen, and Tracy knew what to do. But when she opened Maggie up again, there was far more blood than expected. What was happening? Tracy searched everywhere, yet the source of the flow could not be found. Maggie was bleeding to death. *Please, God, save this dog*, Tracy prayed. She knew there was nothing more she could do.

Suddenly the bleeding stopped. Once again Tracy searched for the source but found nothing—no nicked arteries or loose stitches. Within minutes, Maggie's abdomen was dry. Bewildered, the nurses watched as Tracy—just as puzzled— sewed up Maggie, wrapped her in a warm blanket, and started a blood transfusion. The dog was still alive, but she had been through a lot.

As the hours passed, Maggie ate, drank, and even walked, which were all good signs. But she was still very ill. She had heartworms and intestinal worms, which had led to anemia and liver damage. Her blood couldn't clot, which explained why the bleeding after surgery had been so intense. When Maggie's owners came to pick up the dogs, Tracy explained the situation. The others were ready to go, but Maggie would need some expensive care. "I honestly don't think she'll last through the night," Tracy told Maggie's owners. "Come back tomorrow and we'll see how she's doing."

When Tracy arrived the next morning, she was surprised to find Maggie alive and weakly wagging her tail. The dog had spirit. Maybe she did have some good years ahead, although it was hard to imagine her chances if she was returned to her owners. But the owners never came back, and they ignored the required registered letter from the clinic. Later, their check bounced.

The situation wasn't that unusual. Word had gotten around that Dr. Tracy ran her business on a shoestring, giving discounts to people who couldn't afford treatments and especially promoting early spaying and neutering. So the clinic had become a drop-off for owners who no longer wanted their dogs or cats. Such people would come in acting as if they intended to be regular customers but then never show up to claim their pets after treatment. That was frustrating enough, but Tracy also took on the responsibility of attempting to find homes for abandoned animals before the ten-day waiting period passed. (After ten days, the vet has the option of turning the pet over to rescue groups, finding an adoptive home, or euthanizing it.) It was something she felt she had to do. "Who would take care of the animals if we didn't?"

As the week passed, the staff noticed that despite Maggie's apparently difficult past, she had a sweetly shy disposition, cooperating even during injections or dressing changes. She got to know various people and behaved well when someone familiar was around. "She was really good with children as well as other animals," Tracy says. "She seemed intuitively to know who we accepted, and when we were comfortable."

Maggie was different when she heard loud voices or someone getting hostile. "She was like a lot of good guard dogs," Tracy says. "She'd place herself between us and the source of concern, start a low growl in her throat, and snarl a little." Maggie was not happy about people trying to come into the clinic after hours. (It's a common ploy for thieves to pretend to be "running late" in order to get in and steal drugs.) Maggie would fling herself against the front door while barking and growling, rapidly convincing everyone to come back during regular hours. Given her surprisingly accurate instincts, Tracy began letting Maggie roam freely at night.

But what was she going to do with Maggie? It was difficult to find adoptive homes for guard dogs. There are so many nice, friendly, healthy pets available for adoption; those with aggressive tendencies are often the last to be adopted and the first to be put down. "There's a huge liability problem," Tracy explains. "We and the new owners would be liable if anyone was hurt by the dog. The few people who do want aggressive dogs are often involved in illegal activities and are totally unacceptable adopters." And who would want a dog with Maggie's expensive health problems? The ten-day waiting period was almost over, and Tracy left the clinic that night with a heavy heart. *God,* she found herself praying, *Maggie almost died during her operation. Why did you save her if we're going to have to put her down?*

When she arrived at the clinic the next morning, she still had no answers. But her attention was diverted for a moment by the sight of the front porch. Where were the benches? Strange. Tracy looked around. The door of the garden shed was open, and the tools were gone. Had they been robbed? If someone had gotten inside and stolen drugs or vandalized the equipment, she would be ruined financially. Heart pounding, Tracy unlocked the front door and threw it open. "Everything was just the same as it always was. Nothing disturbed. We were still in business!"

Just then, Tracy heard the thump-thump of Maggie's tail, as the dog came up to be greeted, and suddenly she understood. The only things missing or damaged were the items *outside* the clinic. Nothing had been taken from the inside, because no one had been able to enter. Maggie, protective where her family was concerned, would have seen to that; no doubt she had barked, thrown herself against the door and—in other ways—frightened away any troublemakers. She had become the perfect staff member. Thanks to her, the clinic could go on saving animals.

Today, a computerized system lets vets catch checks before they bounce. In addition, vets have the right to hold an animal until the bill is paid. "This lets us remove animals from bad situations and put them into better ones," Tracy says. Early spaying/neutering is becoming more common, too, and in 2008 Tracy was a top ten finalist and the only vet in Animal Planet's "Hero of the Year" contest. She didn't win but regards it as an honor to be nominated.

And Maggie? She became a healthy protective guardian and a reminder that everyone fits somewhere. God has a plan for even the lowliest of creatures.

Help for a Helper

A really companionable and indispensable dog is an accident of nature. You can't get it by breeding for it, and you can't buy it with money. It just happens along.

—E. B. White, *The Care and Training of a Dog*

As we know, everyone who is in heaven is a saint. But there are also "official" saints, those recognized for all the good they did here on earth. One who probably couldn't have succeeded without a particular heavenly helper was St. John Bosco, mentioned earlier, whose feast day we observe on January 31.

John was born in Becchi, Italy, in 1815, and although he grew up in poverty, he had a terrific mother, who saw that he got an education. Before John had reached his teens, he was already experiencing wonderful nighttime dreams about his future. It seemed clear that he was to become a priest and work with homeless boys, saving them from the streets, educating them, and teaching them about God. Just how all of this was to come about was not explained in the dreams. John set out to accomplish the task anyway.

The street kids that he dealt with were rough, angry, and not all that interested in reforming their lives. Often they would rob John when he approached them. Gradually, he won over the younger ones and established group homes for them. But the assaults continued. And because many of John's rescued boys were hard to handle, the citizenry was not exactly thrilled with his mission. Often, they attempted to drive him out of the area. (Teenagers were considered a supreme annoyance then too!)

One autumn evening in 1852, John was making his way across the most broken part of the slum district. He was alone and depressed. (Yes, even future saints get depressed.) "Lord," he prayed, "I know you want me to care for the least of your children, but I can't go on being mugged and robbed and still do the work you've assigned me. How about a little help?"

Suddenly John noticed a dog behind him. Or was it a wolf? The creature was huge and gray . . . but friendly. Timidly John called it, and the dog trotted up and took his place alongside John, as if he had been trained to do so. "I'll call you Grigio," John told the dog (*Grigio* means "gray" in Italian). The two strolled along in silent companionship until John reached his house, and the dog left, as if his job were done. But it wasn't. A few days later, John had to travel through a dangerous area, where he had once been beaten by street thugs. He was apprehensive but, Grigio showed up again! And again, the canine bodyguard stayed next to John until he reached his home.

Thus began a tender pattern: John walking alone, the dog suddenly appearing and escorting him to safety. On one occasion someone behind a tree fired two shots at John. They missed, and the shooter aimed again. But Grigio raced at him, teeth bared, and the man fled. Another time, as John was walking down a dark and unfamiliar street, two men threw a sack over his head, obviously intending to kill him. Suddenly John heard barking. Yes, although he hadn't seen his faithful companion, here came Grigio again, growling and driving the men away. A few days later, Grigio saved John's life in an attempted ambush. A dozen men had surrounded him with their sticks raised to strike, when Grigio arrived upon the scene. Of course everyone fled.

The gray dog became popular, for he sometimes came into John's house and allowed the smaller boys to play with him. But his appearances always had a purpose. Sometimes it was to meet John at the door before a journey; sometimes to escort John safely home, even when John was unaware of danger. At least once, Grigio even prevented John from going out. He lay down on the threshold and barred the exit. "Grigio, move aside!" John commanded, but the dog resisted, and John eventually gave up and took off his coat. About an hour later, John's neighbor rushed in to warn John that another trap had been set for him. But it had failed, thanks again to Grigio.

By now, John realized that something heavenly was going on. And as if to confirm it, the dog appeared as John was on his way to visit a farmer. When they arrived, John brought the dog inside. Grigio lay down quietly in a corner while the family ate. But when they had assembled leftovers for Grigio's dinner, they could not find him! No doors or windows had been open, yet he had vanished.

For more than thirty years, as John Bosco traveled Italy, saving boys and establishing the Salesian Society, a new order of priests, faithful Grigio continued his inexplicable but wondrous mission (and never grew any older!). To this day, if a Salesian priest is in danger, a large gray dog sometimes appears, just at the right time.

Barbara Johnson had never heard the story of St. John Bosco, at least not at the time she completed her general-nursing training at the Royal Adelaide Hospital in Australia. She worked six months in Melbourne and then went to Sydney to train as a midwife at St. Margaret's Hospital.

Barbara's brother and his wife lived in a suburb of Sydney, so on her first day off, Barbara took the train to their home for a visit. Everyone had a lovely time, and Barbara left for the return journey at about 9 p.m.

"I was feeling proud," she admits. "Although I later got to know the underground subway system well, this was my first time traveling beneath the city. Yet I had found my way around and had gotten off at the right stop." Confidently, she climbed up to a well-lit street and decided to take a shortcut through a park.

Barbara wasn't apprehensive as she began her walk. "I had walked in cities at night and had learned that you keep your pace brisk but not hurried, so onlookers don't think you're afraid." She moved purposefully down the path, and it was only after a few moments that she realized the park was extremely dark inside. Worse, Oxford Street, where the hospital was, seemed much farther away than she had anticipated.

There was no one else in the park, at least no one she could see. But Barbara had the feeling she was being watched. From time to time she saw a glow, like the end of a lit cigarette, in the shadows. Her heart began to pound. She had done a stupid thing and now she was in danger. If someone grabbed her and pulled her into the bushes, there would be little she could do to protect herself. But if she bolted, she could lose her way in the darkness or fall and hurt herself.

There was no choice but to keep going. Barbara quickened her pace and stared straight ahead, fixing her eyes on that distant glow, the streetlights far ahead that signaled safety.

She was about halfway through the park when she sensed movement to her right. Oh, no! As if everything wasn't frightening enough, there was a large Alsatian dog right next to her.

"This breed was very intimidating because the police used them as guard dogs," Barbara says. "They were known to be vicious." Frantically she looked around for the dog's owner, but the park was still deserted. What would she do if the dog charged her? Barbara pictured herself lying bleeding on the dirt, vulnerable to attacks from both man and beast. Tears sprang to her eyes.

But the dog seemed anything but bad tempered. It simply trotted alongside her as if it belonged. Barbara slackened her pace, hoping the furry monster would pass her, but the dog slowed as well. Then she stopped. "Go away, dog." Timidly, she tried to shoo it. "Go away, now!"

But the dog stopped too, as if rooted to the spot, and looked up at her, cocking its massive head. Its demeanor didn't change, and it was not agitated or responsive. It simply *stayed*, like an obedient protector assigned to her side.

Barbara saw no other option but to keep moving, and that's just what she did, almost breaking into a run as she reached the welcome lights of Oxford Street. The dog stood quietly beside her as she glanced down the street to check the traffic. Was it going to follow her across?

Just as she stepped off the curb, Barbara looked to her right once more. The enormous dog was gone.

Relieved, Barbara hurried to the hospital dorm and made herself a cup of tea in the kitchenette. "You look exhausted," one of the nurses said.

"I've had a traumatic experience," Barbara explained. "I took a shortcut just now through the park—"

"You went into the park at night?" another nurse interrupted. "Oh, you're new, you wouldn't have known. But many crimes take place in that park; it's a known drug haven."

Aghast that she had ventured into such a dangerous and poorly lit area, the two nurses related one horror story after another, and Barbara thought back with consternation to the cigarette glows in the shadows. Oh, what might have happened to her! God must have been watching over her.

"And suddenly I was filled with a sense of guardian angels, and I knew without question that the dog had been mine," Barbara says. "There was just no other explanation for his arrival, his behavior, and his sudden disappearance. I felt grateful that God chose to take such personal care of me, and that he is always ready to protect us, even from our own foolishness."

Barbara never saw her angel again, but she named him Guiseppe and feels a bond that has endured through the years.[6]

MORE THAN MAN'S BEST FRIEND

Oh! I have slipped the surly bonds of earth
And danced the skies on laughter-silvered wings . . .

—JOHN GILLESPIE MAGEE, "HIGH FLIGHT"

∞

By the time Gary Lorenz graduated from the Air Force Academy in 1967, he had become not only a full-fledged pilot, but, more important to him, also a good leader. He seemed to have a natural set of values that attracted others, and though somewhat quiet, his look was worth a thousand words. One of the many who were drawn to him was Sandra Clark, and soon they were married. The two began their military life in the Philippines, at the first of fourteen different addresses.

Gary rose through the ranks to become an F-4 pilot and served in Vietnam. Eventually, as a colonel, he became the commanding officer of the strategically important airbase at Incurlik, Turkey. Again, his leadership qualities were evident. At one point, with Desert Storm moving in, Gary wanted to evacuate the American families, but no one in Washington seemed to be listening. One morning, he intercepted the visiting Secretary of State on his morning run. Wearing his dress blues, Gary fell in stride with the Secretary and presented his case. The evacuation was on. "When he was right," said a fellow officer, "Gary would go all out to get things done."

Sandee adjusted to military life, raising their two children and offering fellowship and comfort to the Air Force wives, many of whom were lonely for their families and activities back home. She understood their yearnings because she was a true animal lover and missed riding her own horse, left back in the States. At Incurlik, however, there was a riding stable, and Sandee happily took over temporary guardianship of a horse whose hind legs needed medicating. She and Gary were working on the horse one day when it kicked Gary in the face. He recovered, but the injury would have later significance.

Gary retired with full military honors in 1991, and the couple built their retirement home on 180 acres in the small town of Cotopaxi, Colorado, between Salida and Canon City. The natural beauty and slower pace suited them both, and they enjoyed having animals around again. Gary decided to raise some cattle at first and soon became the neighborhood Pied Piper, leading the herd around the large property by offering them cow treats. Sandee learned to drive an ATV, and she shoveled snow off their long driveway. Probably the best additions to their lives were two golden retrievers that they adopted as puppies from a friend. The goldens were brother and sister, and Gary named them Merry and Pippin, after the two hobbits from the *Lord of the Rings* series. The dogs were friendly to everyone, and they had been unusually docile as puppies, but from the start, Gary was their favorite. "They never left his side," says Deanna Lorenz, Gary's daughter. "They were homebodies too; when they were about six months old, they had gotten lost for a few days, and they never wandered again." Whether Gary went into the house or trod around the trails, the dogs were at his side, not wanting to miss a single minute of whatever was going on.

The family felt that Gary was in good hands. And that was important because he was beginning to show some signs of distress. Deanna noticed that her father fumbled for a word now and then, but she brushed it aside—didn't everyone forget things here and there as they aged? Sandee saw a more specific progression, slow but steady, involving Gary's lack of memory. There was that long-ago kick from the horse—could it have left some lingering damage? Yet when other members of the family came to visit, they saw little or no symptoms.

The women were hesitant to push their observances too firmly. What if they were wrong? But in 2003, Gary's doctor diagnosed him with aphasia, damage to the left frontal lobe where words are formed. He continued to decline, and by 2005 he was an Alzheimer's patient. As the days passed, Gary became more silent. It seemed that only Merry and Pippin were able to understand him.

On Sunday, September 23, 2007, Deanna celebrated her birthday at her grandmother's house in Denver, along with other family members. The following day, she and her mother had an appointment with Gary's doctor to decide if Gary needed to surrender his driver's license. The women knew that he was still capable of driving, but they were worried about him getting involved in an accident with others. Needless to say, they were not looking forward to the appointment.

When the birthday gathering broke up, "I drove home alone with my Dad," Deanna recalls, "and I was happy that we were able to share this time together, even though we couldn't communicate in words. I didn't know it would be the last time."

The following day's appointment was unexpectedly cancelled, because both Deanna and Sandee came down with the flu. Gary, attempting to help, apparently remembered that the horses needed to be fed. But when he went out to drop the hay, the horses had not yet gathered. This was of no real consequence, but Gary took Sandee's four-wheeler to look for them anyway. Merry and Pippin, of course, were following him as they went over a ridge above the house.

Some hours later, when Gary and the dogs had not returned, a worried Sandee called Deanna. "I'm on my way," she reassured her mother and suggested that Sandee phone Debbie, to start getting the word around. Debbie was a friend who knew everyone in town, but the women had forgotten that she was away on a cruise. No matter. When she got the news, Debbie stood on the ship deck and phoned everyone in her cell phone address book to get the search started. It was so effective that by the time Sandee had climbed the hill to start looking around, she encountered a neighbor already walking the paths, checking.

As night fell and volunteers assembled, the Lorenz family fought panic. It was terrifying, knowing that their disoriented father was lost somewhere on the rugged mountain terrain, where there are numerous drop-offs, caves, and canyons. He was wearing light clothes and a sweatshirt too, not enough warmth for the cold nighttime temperatures. There was one hopeful factor: the dogs were probably with Gary. "Merry would never leave Pippin, and Pippin would never leave Gary," Sandee says. It was not too much to hope that, even in his confused state, Gary would show up somewhere, or a searcher would come across a clue and be led to all three of them.

Almost a hundred people turned out on the first few days, and they soon found Gary's ATV at the bottom of a ravine. But where were Gary and the dogs? Despite the diligence of the searchers, along with helicopters sent by the Air Force base, horseback riders, and infrared lights, nothing more turned up.

Some volunteers would later say that they had occasionally heard dogs barking but thought they belonged to a nearby house, and perhaps they did. But too much time had passed. Sandee had to face the fact that her beloved husband was not coming home.

Days dragged by. As hunting season began, Deanna was featured several times on the local radio station. "Don't forget to look for my Dad and the dogs," she reminded listeners. But no responses came. Should the family have a memorial service now or wait in this strange kind of limbo until everything was over? But would it end? Mysteries were not always solved. And what about the dogs? As time passed, and no golden made his weary way out of the woods to their home, their grief deepened. Weeks of searching had turned up nothing. On October 9, the search was officially discontinued.

In the end, it was a hunter who found Gary's body. He and his buddies came to this same location each year, and on the first day, the hunter set out alone against a stiff wind. "Before I lost complete cell contact, I phoned my wife, and we talked for a few moments about the beauty of the surrounding area," Pat says. In a later letter to Sandee, he traced the route he'd taken, following deer up the mountainside. Was he hearing some faint barking?

Pat continued to work his way around a high ridge, and suddenly a thin but beautiful golden retriever bounded up to him in friendly fashion. Then Pat remembered something, and using his walkie-talkie, he radioed his buddies. "That fellow they told us about, the one that's been lost, did he own a golden retriever?"

"Two retrievers," came the answer.

By now, Merry was barking at Pat, her tail wagging furiously. It was as if she was begging him to follow her. Pat did, and she scrambled down the ridge about thirty yards. Pippin then came into view, barking loudly. Next to Pippin, Pat could see what everyone had been searching for during the last several weeks. He hit the switch again. "I think I found all of them."

For the next three hours, Pat stayed on his cell phone (which, remarkably, still had power) as he directed the sheriff and 911 dispatchers to his location. "During that time I attempted to feed the dogs with a half a sandwich I had in my pocket," Pat told Sandee, "but neither of them would leave

Gary's side. Finally Merry came over and took a piece of bread, and later, I brought her some water." Pippin, however, refused to move away from Gary, and when searchers finally arrived, he snarled and continued to bark until he recognized one of the neighbors.

"I was touched by the love and loyalty the dogs showed for Colonel Lorenz," Pat says. "At one point, Merry came over and buried her head in my lap, as if to express her sorrow. I could see the sadness in her eyes."

Neighbors brought the stunning news to Sandee and Deanna. "Gary's been found. And the dogs —the dogs are alive!" The women could not believe it. The dogs must have been with Gary when he died. Had Merry and Pippin kept their lonely vigil for another three weeks, guarding his body, never leaving his side?

As details emerged, the family learned that Gary was discovered almost four miles (by a bird's flight) from his home. Helicopters had flown over that area several times, but he was lying under a tree, partially hidden by a rock. The dogs were probably leaning up against him, attempting to keep him warm. The coroner later confirmed that Gary had died of hyperthermia and dehydration on September 29, five days after he disappeared.

Five days! It was heartbreaking to imagine how Gary had probably struggled to find his way back. And yet as Sandee opened her arms to receive the dogs, she could not help but be grateful that they had survived. In many ways, they were a part of her husband.

But *how* had they survived? No food, no water for almost a month. The dogs were emaciated and ravenous when they were returned to Sandee, and each had lost nine pounds. She fed them a small amount every few hours at first, so they wouldn't overeat. Merry had a slight limp, and Pippin—at one time a clown—was more aggressive than usual. But their vet pronounced both dogs amazingly fit.

Gary Lorenz's funeral mass attracted hundreds of mourners and was held at the Air Force Academy's Cadet Chapel on October 29, 2007. He received full military honors at the graveside service. The American flag was folded and presented to Sandee. Deanna spoke of the remarkable life her father had lived. "If you want to know what kind of person a man is," she told the crowd, "ask his dog."

Lying quietly on either side of the casket, wearing black scarves around their necks, Merry and Pippin gave testimony to Deanna's words. They were calm, gazing serenely at the crowd, yet at the end of the ceremony, both dogs seemed bewildered and had to be gently urged away. It was finally time to let go.

Sandee believes that had the hunter not found them, the dogs would have stayed with Gary until they took their last breath. "To know that Merry and Pippin were with him when he passed from this world to the next, that he wasn't alone, means everything to me," she says.

And Deanna has observed something wondrous as well. "When Merry was returned to us, I realized that her face was no longer golden," Deanna says. "It had turned completely white."

The touch of an angel? Someday we'll know.

NOTHING TO SNIFF AT

We may be sent by God to save animals, but in reality,
they are sent to save us too.

—PETWARMERS.COM

⤬

On a cold wintry day several years ago, Mary Ellen Anderson put three-year-old Scott in the car and drove to pick up her daughter Kim from kindergarten, an errand she and little Scott did every day. It was overcast and gray, and Mary Ellen was glad she had some shopping to do. She and her family lived in a rural community not too far from Kokomo, Indiana, and days could go by without her seeing a neighbor or friend. Sometimes the indoor mall was her only change of scene in this long monotonous winter.

The children were cooperative and cheerful at the mall, but eventually Mary Ellen looked outside and realized that it had started to rain, the freezing kind that often turns to snow and makes driving a nightmare. "Kids," she announced, "we'd better start for home."

There was a thin sheet of ice already forming in the parking lot; Mary Ellen tried to keep the three of them upright. Cautiously they made their way to the car, and she buckled both of the children into the front passenger seat as she usually did. They were so little that both could fit inside one belt. Scott was smaller, so he sat next to Mary Ellen, with Kim nearest the door. (This is not permitted today, but it was legal then.)

"By this time I realized that we had a problem," Mary Ellen says. "The rain had turned to a slippery sleet on the road, and I needed gas." There was a little crossroads town a mile or two ahead that had a small gas station. It was one of the few buildings that had survived a recent tornado, and Mary Ellen wasn't sure it was still in business. But her car was sliding uncontrollably and she had to take a break. There was the station up ahead, completely deserted. She let the car slow itself, and "I eased into the station, going about five miles an hour. But when I braked, nothing happened. I turned the wheel quickly, and the steering wouldn't work either!" With no other options, Mary Ellen's car crashed into one of the two gasoline pumps and knocked it over. The next thing she saw were flames shooting upward.

The front of her car was on fire! She had to get the children out, and she reached quickly for the seatbelt buckle. But her fingers simply would not work! Trembling, she tried to pull Scott up and out of the belt but it was too tight. "Oh God, please . . ." Mary Ellen tugged on the buckle and prayed in the shorthand known to all parents. The fire seemed so close! Just then the belt released, and she dragged Scott across her lap and out of her open door. "Run, honey!" she told him.

She reached for Kim as Scott's little legs went out from under him and he fell. There was a coating of heavy ice over the entire station, on the building, the pumps, and worst of all, on the cement. Scott couldn't run on it. As Mary Ellen set Kim on the cement, her daughter's feet slipped, and she, too, lost her balance. Scott was trying to stand, but he couldn't. Kim couldn't run either! Mary Ellen unbuckled herself, lunged out of her car door, and took a step toward her children, both scrambling to get up. Instead, she slipped and went down on one knee. *There's going to be an explosion*, she thought in panic. *And we can't do anything about it.*

Then, as if a movie were playing right in front of Mary Ellen, she saw a dog—a very large dog, standing in the middle of the station, looking at her. "He was about the size and appearance of an English sheepdog. Shaggy, kind of a dirty white color and unkempt." Where had he come from? Mary Ellen had always had a fear of dogs and had tried not to pass it on to her children. But now, as Kim struggled to her feet again, Mary Ellen saw her reach for the dog, grabbing his thick fur for balance.

Far from being aggressive, the dog seemed calm, patiently waiting as if he were on an assignment. Scott saw his sister clinging to the dog, and he reached out to do the same. The dog trotted toward him, paws steady on the ice, and waited almost passively until Scott had a good grip on his fur. Then the dog headed for the small building on the premises, dragging both children away from the flames. They clung to him as if he were pulling them in a wagon, slipping and sliding along, all perfectly choreographed. Shakily, Mary Ellen got to her feet again and started to follow them.

By now an employee had come out of the building to see what was happening. "Hey, lady!" he called to Mary Ellen, "it's okay. Your car's not on fire."

Couldn't he see the flames? She felt again a sense of unreality. But the man was explaining something to her. The flames shooting up from the hole in the ground where the pump had been were between the bumper and the front of the car. The car itself had not caught on fire, at least not yet.

Relief flooded her. The children were safe; she could see them standing by the door of the building. The flames were dying down. And now the garage employee was pushing her car out of the pump area. There would be minimal damage, he told her. She and the children had had a "lucky break" and all was well.

Because of the dog. He had arrived at the perfect time, but in this deserted area, where did he live? She looked over at her children. The dog was nowhere to be seen. And he wasn't trotting away from the scene.

"Kids, what happened to that white dog?"

"I don't know," Kim answered, looking around. "I guess he's gone."

Wouldn't the attendant have seen the dog as he ran toward them? And yet, through the unreality of it all, a solid conclusion emerged. No ordinary dog could have arranged such a perfect way to rescue two endangered children. And hadn't he arrived just moments after she prayed?

She would have quite a story to tell her husband that evening.

NEW LEASHES ON LIFE

My dogs have been scamps and thieves and troublemakers,
and I've adored them all.

—HELEN HAYES

⟡

It may seem unbelievable, especially to those without pets, but in times of approaching disasters, some people will not leave their homes if they cannot take their pets with them. In fact, a Zogby International study found that 44 percent of those who stayed behind when Hurricane Katrina hit did so because they wouldn't abandon Fido or Fluffy. This decision, although understandable, puts everyone involved at risk. That's why people involved in large-scale rescue missions emphasize the necessity of having some kind of pet disaster plan and a kit that contains food and water, photos, and medications, so they can "grab and go." Owners should also have the names of a few pet-friendly motels near the evacuation route because many accommodations do not accept animals.

Karen O'Toole of Paradise Valley, Arizona, has seen more of these situations than she cares to remember. She's always had a heightened sensitivity to the smaller living things around us, she says; as a child she worried about inadvertently crushing ants under her feet, and she buried dead birds with tears flowing. "When I meet someone who has never had pets, or who doesn't like animals, I feel sorry for them," she says. "They are missing out on one of the greatest pleasures on earth."

Thus it was not surprising that Karen ultimately became involved in pet rescues. As an award-winning Hollywood writer and production coordinator, she also started a Web site where rescuers share information. It was not surprising that, when she heard about Katrina and the devastation left in its wake, she was almost first on the scene. "I had seen one too many pictures on television of people hanging out of attics and abandoned pets everywhere," she says. "I had to go." Armed with a crowbar and her usual determination, she navigated her way into the center of the disaster.

"My first view was a wet dog standing on a truck roof, imprisoned by the rushing water. He barked but camera crews went right by." It appeared that no one was going to save Louisiana's pets. It was up to Karen and her colleagues. Little did she know that she would end up living and working for three months in the parking lot of a grocery store.

Today the emphasis on lost or homeless animals is to attempt to rescue them for ultimate adoption, rather than putting them to sleep. "Rescuing" does not only mean simply catching the stray but also following through with whatever he needs: searching for his original family, spaying, attending to medical needs, microchipping, and even administering a temperament test. Healthy animals are then easier to find homes for, and their owners usually understand the need to "fix" them to prevent population growth.

As everyone agrees, animal-loving volunteers are the life blood of this movement. Some are actual rescuers, others donate hours at the shelters, and some foster animals for a time, until a permanent home is found. And such work is far more fruitful now that people can connect via the Internet. Rescuers communicate through e-mails and Web sites and can often hook up a rescuer halfway across the country with an animal that needs some help.

When pet rescuers go into an area, there's no set format. They simply look for animals in distress and attempt to meet the situation in some way. They talk to everyone they can, keep notes on people who are sympathetic, or who have a place for an ailing animal, or groups who will perhaps contribute food and other items, or who can drive animals to safer areas. Much of their work is a step of faith. So it was in New Orleans. "I cannot describe the time I spent there rescuing animals—and not rescuing them," says Karen. "So many were missed. And for others, we were just too late." Those who didn't drown frequently died of starvation, for there wasn't a morsel of food anywhere. "Everything in the city was rancid, waterlogged, and decayed. We were a handful of people trying to rescue a city of pets. As hard as we worked, there were not enough of us. There could never be enough of us."

And yet, as always, good things happened. There were tiny bits of encouragement and some amazing "coincidences."

One day Karen was working in the parking lot headquarters when a young pregnant woman approached her. The girl was leading a beautiful black-and-white dog that had the look of a border collie. "I'm Tami, and this is Sasha," she told Karen. "You're one of those pet rescuers, aren't you?"

"Yes, I am."

"I've just gotten into a FEMA trailer, but they won't take dogs," Tami explained, her voice quivering. "I've only had Sasha for a few months, and she's a good friend. She's been living in my car, but . . ." Tears spilled out of her eyes. Sasha reached up and licked Tami's cheeks. Her eyes were filled with sympathy, as if she were the caretaker instead of the other way around. "She needs a real home, but I'd like her to stay in the city so I could visit her," Tami continued. "Can you do that for her?"

Karen didn't know what to say. How could she promise a home for this dog when everyone in the city seemed to be homeless? But that was what her volunteer job involved. She would have to try.

The two women and Sasha went over to the FEMA trailer park, and Karen started making phone calls to numbers she had jotted down on slips of paper. The tow truck driver who wanted to lend a hand, a volunteer she had met this morning in a parking lot . . . "I have this beautiful and gentle dog that needs a home," Karen said over and over again. It seemed that no one could help. Then Karen connected with a friend of a friend of a friend. "Her name is Tina, and she lives in Plaquemine Parish, about twenty-five miles from here," Karen told Tami. "But it's not in the city."

Tami knew Plaquemine was rural and one of the most decimated areas, not what she had hoped for. But she was aware of how difficult the search was. "Go ahead and call" she told Karen. "We have to try."

But Tina, this unknown Good Samaritan, was dead set against taking Sasha. "I lost a dog of my own, Gabby, about six months ago," she explained over the phone to Karen. "I looked everywhere, but once the hurricane hit, I had to face the fact that she was probably dead. You know how that hurts. And now I've lost some horses, and my house is mostly destroyed." Tina was almost ready to hang up. Tami could hear part of the conversation, and she looked desperately at Karen.

"Maybe just for a little while?" Karen pleaded, her heart starting to pound. "She's a lovely well-behaved dog."

There was a silence. Then Tina sighed. "Well, I guess it wouldn't hurt to foster her for a few weeks."

"That's wonderful!" Karen was overjoyed. Despite her problems, Tina had a warm manner, and Karen's intuition told her that Sasha would be safe and loved. Karen also sensed another positive feeling, something hovering just outside her grasp, but there was no time to ponder. Quickly they arranged to meet. Sasha needed to join her new caretaker before Tina changed her mind!

It took almost an hour to get there because the roads were still difficult to navigate, but eventually Karen, Tami, and Sasha pulled up at the meeting place. A woman (Tina) started toward them. Karen reached across the front seat where Sasha had been snoozing and opened the passenger door. Sasha awakened, yawned, and got to her feet. When she saw Tina, she tensed up. Then she started to bark—and continued to bark. Karen grabbed the leash before the dog could scramble out of the car. Sasha was straining at the leash, yet she seemed *ecstatic*, rather than upset. And then Tina screamed with joy.

"Gabby! Gabby!" She ran to the dog with her arms outstretched. "It's Gabby!" She looked at Karen, her eyes shining. "This is my dog, my Gabby! You brought her back to me!"

Karen released the leash, and Gabby leaped out of the car and up against Tina. Tina buried her face in the dog's fur. "Gabby, Gabby," She kept murmuring. Karen and Tami were speechless. Given all the stray dogs in Louisiana, how could this have happened? If Tina had refused to reach out, if she had decided to be practical instead of loving, it *wouldn't* have happened. Everything had had to go right for this strange and wonderful connection to happen.

Perhaps this was what Karen had sensed as she started the drive to meet Tina. Had that unexpected feeling of well-being been a message from the heavens, encouraging her to keep trying, despite the impossible odds?

Gabby/Sasha was still barking, still leaping joyfully. Karen reached for her car keys. There were a lot more animals waiting for her.

Kristin Hubbard of Charlotte, North Carolina, is a friend of Karen's and has the same dedication. She was raised with many animals, since her mother rescues cocker spaniels and her father does the same for Great Danes. (At one point the family had twelve dogs and more than thirty cats.) "It's in my blood," she admits. In fact, today Kristin is also a freshwater turtle rescuer/rehabilitator licensed by the state. So it was not unusual for her to get an occasional e-mail from a friend here or there, looking for a temporary home for a distressed animal. For several years she drove rescue transports on weekends despite her busy schedule raising four children under the age of twelve, a Lab/husky mix named Bear, five cats, and a dozen or so turtles.

One morning a volunteer sent out an e-mail: workers had found a dog in a commercial dumpster, along with nine puppies, four of them already dead. Manning the phone lines, they had managed to find homes for the remaining puppies, but the mother, whom they named Molly and seemed to be primarily a Staffordshire terrier, was emaciated beyond belief. She had obviously been dumped there to die and would be put down the next day unless someone stepped up to foster her.

At first Kristin had reservations about taking the dog. Garrison, her three-year-old, had been recently diagnosed with autism. Although it had not come as a complete surprise—Garrison was almost completely nonverbal and disinterested in the animals—Kristin was still reeling from the news. Would she have the patience and the time to devote to a new dog? "Then I took one look at the photo they provided, and that was it," Kristin says. "If nothing else, I could let her die with some dignity and peace."

The family took Molly in and introduced her to everyone. "Bear has his own bed," Kristin says, "and as soon as we brought Molly in, he got up, sniffed and greeted her, and then lay down *next* to his bed, so I could put Molly on it." (Bear is an amazingly intuitive dog, the family says; almost like a human in a dog's body.) After eating and being coaxed outside that first day, Molly climbed into Bear's bed and went to sleep. "Hard sleep," Kristin recalls. "Snoring and twitching and dead-to-the-world sleep." This pattern went on for about three days: eating, going outside, and returning to heavy sleep, while the household watched. (All except Garrison.) Finally it seemed that they had crossed some kind of barrier. When Molly did awaken, she was a new creation, even waving her helicopter swirl tail as family members approached. Kristin felt certain that time would eventually erase her bad memories.

For the next few days Molly explored her home, making friends with the cats and gradually learning to throw a ball back and forth with four-year-old Jake. However, more than any of the others, Molly wanted to be friends with Garrison. She followed him around the house, accepting his indifference but continuing to wave her tail in his direction and getting no response. Of course the dog had no way of knowing that Garrison didn't speak. Would this become a problem?

A few nights later, Kristin served pizza for dinner. Garrison had just started eating when Molly quickly approached him. Kristin started toward Molly. It seemed obvious that the dog was going to take the pizza away from Garrison, but she didn't. Instead she settled at his feet, just firmly enough to let everyone know that she was "on the job."

The next morning Garrison came to the breakfast table and stopped when he saw Molly. As Kristin watched, he went over to the dog, put his hands gently on either side of her face, and said, very clearly, "Hi, Molly!"

"It was a moment I will never forget as long as I live," Kristin says. "Molly just licked him and wagged that tail of hers. It was amazing."

Today Molly is the picture of health, having doubled her weight. She greets visitors with a friendly wave, then sits and puts her paw up to shake. She has established herself as a "Mama's girl" too, cuddling at Kristin's feet more often than not. Surprisingly, Molly is also extremely athletic. "She can leap six-foot fences in a single bound," says Kristin, "and can jump almost ten feet in the air from a sitting position. She has muscles on her muscles!"

But Molly's favorite activity continues to be spending time with both boys, especially Garrison. Garrison is still nonverbal, but now he hugs Molly all the time, especially around her middle, and she wags and smiles (in dog language). Garrison now pays a lot of attention to the household menagerie, which currently includes four dogs and ten cats. He leaves no doubt that there is plenty of communication going on.

And Kristin? She blesses the day that she reached out to a throwaway dog. How could she have known that it would be one of the best decisions she's ever made?

BREANA'S BABY

The little dog laughed, to see such sport...

—"HEY DIDDLE, DIDDLE," NURSERY RHYME

Stories in books like these tend to gloss over the downside of having a dog, that is, the patience required to train it so that it will be a cherished and well-disciplined member of the family. Many a dog is labeled "incorrigible" (and sometimes abandoned) simply because no one has been willing or able to train him. Those who foster abused and unwanted pets— and often try to teach them some manners—must be angels in disguise.

Breana Bartholomew, an accountant in San Jose, California, has done dog fostering and rescuing in the past. But when she was laid off, she had to cut back financially and now had just two elderly dogs. "I'm not a puppy person," she admits. "Sure, they're cute, but wayyyyyyy too much work. Whenever I have counseled people about adopting a dog, I always bring up the issues of house-breaking, chewing, and obedience training; do they really have the time and desire to go through all of that?" Most "problem dogs" under the age of two are dumped for being out of control. But older dogs are past these problems and indeed seem to show more love and appreciation for having been rescued and given a second chance.

A few days before Christmas 2009, Breana and her roommate noticed a small black-and-white border collie running loose across the street. Traffic is heavy, and the pup could easily be hit by a car. "I'll see if I can catch it," Breana's roommate announced, and he went out to access the situation. Not good. Whenever he approached, the dog would run away. After an hour of trying, he gave up. "Think you can do it?" he asked, still concerned about the dog's safety

Breana suspected that the puppy had been abused by a man; hence its reluctance to come to her roommate. And it *was* a puppy, the very age she didn't want to handle. But she couldn't simply walk away. (Actually, she *could*, but that's why rescuers are special people.) Instead, she went across the street with some doggie treats, but the dog would not be coaxed out of the bushes. "She was exhausted, barely keeping her eyes open," Breana says. "She had tags on her collar, so I assume she belonged to someone in the neighborhood." The dog wouldn't meet Breana's eyes, which indicated that she was, indeed, afraid, so Breana sat on the grass about three feet away, slowly breaking off pieces of the treats and tossing them closer and closer to her. "After a while, I left to go get her some water," says Breana. "When I came back, she was standing near the street, looking for me."

For the next hour, Breana talked softly to the pup. Finally it nibbled a treat from Breana's outstretched hand, and she was able to read the name on the collar: "Panda." "I started calling her by name," Breana says. "It was getting late in the afternoon, so I stood up and said 'C'mon Panda, let's go!' and tried to cross the street, hoping she would follow." She did not.

Breana went home to get more treats. This time when she returned, Panda was standing at the edge of the street. Once again they went through the routine, but Breana was getting discouraged. Panda must belong to someone nearby, and hopefully she would go home. "So, I got up and crossed the street.

I didn't look back because I felt guilty for leaving her." When she went in the house, her roommate, who had been watching the drama, shook his head. "How did you do that?"

"Do what?" Breana asked. The roommate pointed. Panda had followed Breana across the street and was sitting on their lawn.

Now a new routine began: Breana on her porch, leaving the front door open, going into the house, calling Panda, coming out with more treats or water, going back in the house again. Slowly, slowly Panda climbed the stairs, peeked inside, then scampered back to the lawn. The performance went on and on, but Panda refused to come inside. By now it was getting dark and cold, and Breana was ready to give up. "Papa" (her name for God), she prayed silently, "if you want me to help Panda, you need to send her into the house *right now.*" As if on cue, Panda suddenly trotted up the porch stairs and through the front door, wagging her tail. Three hours of kindness and love had turned her from a frightened stray into a perky pup. But, at about eight months old, not a very well-behaved one.

Chaos reigned almost immediately. "As I suspected, Panda was not only a chewer (she started in on my late father's recliner!), but she was also terrible on a leash," Breana says.

"When she encountered other dogs while we were walking, she'd go crazy, leaping in the air, barking like the enemy had just landed and she was late for the fight!" Panda would sit on command, but she would not stay. She dropped balls rather than returning them and even learned to jump Breana's six-foot fence. Was the dog dumb or stubborn? Breana couldn't decide.

She had phoned the number on Panda's tags, but there was no answer. She ran ads in the papers, on the Humane Society's Web site, and on Craigslist, but no one responded. Some days, deep in depression over her unemployment situation, Breana would talk to God while she walked her "wild child." "Papa, you know I wanted another Doberman, not a young pup! Please help me find a good home for Panda." Breana also added "Grace" to Panda's name. Despite the mischief and mayhem she caused, Breana thought maybe the dog was a sign of God's grace to her, in a way she didn't yet understand.

"I hung on to Panda, praying for help and thinking maybe I'd give her to border collie rescue when the economy got a little better," she says. "My other dogs, a Lab almost sixteen years old, and a chow mix that was ten, accepted Panda Grace but were a little overwhelmed by her exuberance." In fact,

Breana couldn't take Panda anywhere in polite society. The dog's frisky aggressiveness was sure to create problems. Due to the arthritis in her hands, Breana had even purchased a stronger leash, but it was of little help. *Why me? Why a puppy?* She often asked herself as she ran to keep up with Panda.

One day, instead of another solitary walk, Breana headed for a local dog park. If she kept Panda outside of the wire fence, perhaps the puppy would get the idea that dogs were supposed to like each other. Sure enough, the other dogs yipped and gathered at the wire fence to meet a new comrade. Panda lunged and attempted to bite their noses. "No! Be Nice!" Breana yelled, pulling back on the leash and apologizing to the owners.

Inga, a woman who owned a young German shepherd named Molly, volunteered to take Molly over to the smaller dog area, which was unoccupied, to let Panda get used to another dog. Breana hesitated. What if Panda harmed Molly? Inga was convinced it would be fine, so the two women took the dogs into the other area and let them off their leashes.

Molly was thrilled and wanted to play. Panda was terrified and kept running away. "Finally, we threw balls for the dogs, and Panda caught a few," Breana recalls. "Even better, she let Molly catch a few. There was no fighting, no growling. I was amazed!" Perhaps Panda's reaction to other dogs, her get-you-before-you-get-me attitude had been based on fear, Breana realized. Rather than fighting, she was now lying on the grass, looking at Molly, and then at Breana, trying to figure out what to do next. Breana was thrilled. Panda had behaved herself!

Panda Grace now visits the park on a regular basis and, for the most part, behaves very well, even showing off a little as she jumps to grab a ball. Recently two new dogs came up to get acquainted, and instead of striking a combative pose, Panda bumped noses with each of them (or is that flirting?). She's calmer, Breana says, and far more trusting of people, especially men. She now sleeps with Breana ("which is a comfort to me except when I get a paw in the face"). And with extra lattice installed, Panda no longer can jump Breana's backyard fence. In fact, she doesn't even try.

"Only the dear Lord knows where this is all going to go," Breana says. "Maybe Panda will stay with me, or maybe I'm just here to 'straighten' her out before she finds her forever home. Maybe the meaning of persevering through such a difficult time is just that—being thankful for the ability to keep my home and dogs and to truly learn the meaning of faith, that all will work out in the end.

"I have to admit, her smiling face is a welcome sight during these stressful times. I think angels come in many forms, including four legs and fur."

Angel in the Cemetery

Seventy-one-year-old William Doubler's family was shocked when he was diagnosed with colon cancer in November and given six months to live. William and his wife were people of great faith. "We set up a hospice for Dad at their home," says their daughter, Mary Frank, "and each day I would come in and we'd have a prayer vigil. Even though there was great pain at the thought of losing him, there was more pain as we watched his suffering increase." That was why, when William died only six weeks after his diagnosis, Mary felt relief as well as loss.

"None of us were expecting it," she says. "We had planned a last Christmas together, and now even that wouldn't happen."

Everyone in their close-knit family grieved, but Mary's younger sister, Marilyn Wakenight, was inconsolable. "I was sick a lot when I was little," Marilyn says, "and Dad was my constant companion. As I grew, I became a tomboy and accompanied Dad while he did chores. I just couldn't imagine life without him."

It was a somber Christmas. The Doubler family had decided to hold the funeral services over until the following week, so that the out-of-town relatives and friends could observe Christmas with their own families. It was a considerate gesture, but it also had the effect of keeping everyone in a state of intense mourning. Marilyn wept constantly, and Mary began to worry about her. Marilyn hadn't been able to attend the family prayer vigils, to prepare as the others had. She needed a sign that Dad had not left them forever. In fact, they all needed a sign.

William was waked on Friday afternoon and evening, and Marilyn went back to the funeral home after everyone had left, to spend some quiet time with her father. The funeral was on

Saturday, and afterward the Doublers hosted a luncheon for all the family and guests. Again, Marilyn slipped away. Where was she going now? Mary wondered, concerned. She was just about to send out some people to look for Marilyn when she reappeared at the luncheon. Mary was surprised. Her sister looked almost happy.

"You've got to see this!" Marilyn announced to the remaining group. "There is a dog lying on top of Dad's grave! When he saw me, he jumped up and kept on licking my face. I want to take him something to eat—he looks like he's hungry." She gathered a plate of meat and other tidbits. Mary looked at her mother, and both women reached for their coats. If a stray dog would make Marilyn feel better, they'd encourage her.

In the freezing afternoon, eight people drove to the cemetery. "And as Marilyn had described, there was a dog lying on top of Dad's grave," Mary says. "He looked like a large mixed-breed collie, red, brown, and white, and he didn't have a collar or tags. When Marilyn got out of the car and climbed the hill to Dad's grave, the dog jumped up and down, wagged his tail, and licked her all over. She couldn't help but laugh! That dog was so loving, and so excited to see her."

And yet there was something surreal about the scene. Given that the day was bitterly cold, why would a dog stay out in the open on top of a hill? There were fir trees nearby, where he could have gone to be sheltered from the wind. And instead of lying on his side, the dog had been covering the grave with his body, his head on the ground as if he were a sentinel guarding it.

"That's strange," Marilyn's mother murmured, looking intently at the dog.

"What, Mom?" Marilyn asked.

"That dog. He looks exactly like Rusty."

"Who's Rusty?"

"He was your father's dog. The first one we ever had on the farm. They could be twins."

Marilyn looked back at the dog. By now everyone wanted to pet him, but he wouldn't have it. He ducked away from the outstretched hands, instead dancing in circles around Marilyn, his eyes searching her face as if he were performing just for her, his tail fanned out in the wind. It was obvious to everyone there that he had chosen Marilyn to love.

The women left him a plate of food that night. "We went back in the morning," Mary says, "and sure enough, he was still protecting my dad's grave. We got out of the car and again, it was my sister that the dog chose. He lavished her with kisses, all over her face. He wagged his tail. He ran circles around her, excited as if she was a long-lost friend." He would have nothing to do with Mary, even though she had a large piece of meat in her hand for him.

The women left him another plate of food and some water. Marilyn went back three times that day to see him. Mary noticed that her sister's misery seemed to be lifting just a little.

That night the women phoned their neighbors, asking if anyone had a dog like the one at the cemetery. No one within a five-mile radius recognized his description. "I'm going to take him home," Marilyn told Mary. "It's so cold, and he obviously doesn't have a place to go."

"And he certainly loves you!" Mary added. The dog still had eyes only for Marilyn. There seemed to be a special bond between them, one that neither woman had ever experienced. If Marilyn took him home, it would be a perfect solution.

But the next day, the dog was gone. As quickly as he had come, he vanished.

Marilyn came back from the cemetery with the news. She had called and whistled and walked the entire area, but there was no sign of the dog. Could he have decided to go back to his earlier home? Both women went back to the snow-covered hill. As Marilyn had said, the dog was gone. *Come back,* Mary whispered to him. *Come back and give my sister some hope.* They had just started to recover from their father's death, and now the grieving would begin anew. "Where could he have gone?" Marilyn asked, bewildered. "And why?"

The answer came suddenly to Mary, the words a blessing. "Do you remember that passage from the Apostle's Creed?" she asked Marilyn. "The one that says, 'On the third day He rose again from the dead'?"

Marilyn met her eyes. "It's the third day since we saw the dog, isn't it? Do you suppose he came to guide Dad to heaven?"

Mary had no doubt. Her father had known how devastated his daughter was and had arranged for a special angel to come and ease her mourning. God took what had been a hard time for them and turned it into a miracle.

The dog never reappeared, but the Doubler family knows where he is. They look forward to seeing him—and their father—again.

Final Thoughts

Because she walks with her daughter every morning, my friend Mary Katherine Kelly Siatta has had an opportunity to observe the playful actions of her daughter's two dogs, especially the younger. When Mary Katherine opens the front door of her daughter's house, this puppy comes running, squealing, and doing backflips, ecstatic at the mere appearance of Mary Katherine. "She licks my face, runs in circles, and can hardly hold still to let me pet her," MK says. "The thing about dogs is they love you that much no matter what you have done, how you look, or how badly you have messed up. It makes my morning."

One day as the dog danced in delight, a thought occurred to Mary Katherine. This is how she—all of us—should be toward God. We should be as blissful as a puppy every time we approach him, thrilled to be spending some time with him.

Suddenly a new voice entered her thoughts, and she knew it was God. *Oh no, you have it wrong. I am the puppy!* he said. *This is how excited I get when you spend time with me. This is how much joy I feel because of my complete and unconditional love for you. So come away and be with me often. Give yourself to me and increase my delight.*

It sounds like fun, doesn't it? Called into the presence of our Father, playing with him with happy abandon, enjoying the moment, and asking for nothing more than his attention, his smile.

Do we really have to wait until eternity for this? Or could we bring that joy to everyone we meet, sharing our gratitude and enthusiasm, seeking out the positive parts of life, and celebrating them no matter how tiny? With each laugh, the world itself will be transformed.

I've heard it before, and it must be true: We can learn a lot about God from a dog.

Recommended Reading

Anderson, Allen and Linda. *Angel Dogs: Divine Messengers of Love.* Novato, CA: New World Library, 1995.

Anderson, Allen and Linda. *Dogs and the Women Who Love Them.* Novato, CA: New World Library, 2010.

O'Toole, Karen. *Orphans of Katrina.* Carefree, AZ: Give a Dog a Bone Press, 2010.

Tompkins, Ptolemy. *The Divine Life of Animals.* New York: Crown Publishers, 2010.

Notes

1. "Canine Sentries" was originally published in *Angels and Wonders* (Chicago: Loyola Press, 2008).

2. "To Sir, with Love" was originally published in *The Power of Miracles* (Chicago: Loyola Press, 2005).

3. "Views from the Bridge" (Part one) was originally published in *Angels and Wonders* (Chicago: Loyola Press, 2008).

4. Taken from *The Charity Letters of JoAnn Cayce*, which can be ordered for $22.00 from Bright Cloud Press, 5128 B. Street, Little Rock, Ark. 72205.

5. Authors Bob and Cheryl Moeller have a national marriage ministry featuring a TV show, radio show, and conferences for married couples and singles with the purpose of connecting two hearts for a lifetime.
www.forkeepsministries.com
forkeepsministries@gmail.com

6. "Help for a Helper" (Part Two) was originally published as "Watcher in the Woods" in *Where Angels Walk* (Sea Cliff, NY: Barton & Brett Publishers, 1992).